German Poetry of the Romantic Era
An Anthology

German Poetry
of the Romantic Era

An Anthology

EDITED & INTRODUCED BY

Osman Durrani

OSWALD WOLFF BOOKS
BERG PUBLISHERS
Leamington Spa / New York

© Copyright Osman Durrani 1986

British Library Cataloguing in Publication Data

German Poetry of the Romantic era : an anthology.
1. German poetry
I. Durrani, Osman
831'.7'08   PT1172

ISBN 0–907582–80–X
ISBN 0–907582–81–8 Pbk

Published in 1986 by **Berg Publishers Ltd**
24 Binswood Avenue, Leamington Spa, CV32 5SQ UK
175 Fifth Avenue, New York 10010, New York, USA

Printed in Great Britain at the University Printing House, Oxford

Contents

Notes

Textual Note

This collection makes no claim to put forward a definitive text of the poems, a task best reserved for the compilers of the historical-critical editions of the German Romantics. A number of these are currently in progress; the critical apparatus appended to them yields some insight into the complexity of their editors' labours. Many of the poems in the present anthology exist in several distinct versions: in isolated manuscripts, among the author's private jottings and correspondence, in ephemeral journals, within novels such as *Godwi* and *Ahnung und Gegenwart*, in collections of *Lieder*, as well as in the numerous authorised and unauthorised editions of the poet's works. Textual variants, alternative titles, and occasionally even major revisions will be encountered when comparing these sources. Different editions of the same poet therefore inevitably contradict each other in matters of detail — witness the variations in the texts established by the *Düsseldorfer Ausgabe* and the *Säkularausgabe* of Heine. At the other extreme, many current editions produced in Germany for the non-specialist are in a standardised form that largely ignores the orthography and punctuation used by the poet. My own versions derive from a consideration of the scholarly editions cited in my notes, but where differing manuscript and published versions are extant, the final choice was necessarily a subjective one. At all times I was guided by the following principles: firstly, to preserve, when possible, the text of one version authorised by the poet during his lifetime; secondly, to observe the spelling reforms that turned 'Thaten' into 'Taten', 'gieb' into 'gib', and 'frey' into 'frei'; thirdly, to retain the author's punctuation as far as practicable; and fourthly, to reduce the number of optional apostrophes in syncopated words ('heil'ge') whose meaning is unambiguous. If I have been inconsistent in so doing, I hope I was no more so than the poets themselves and perhaps less so than their contemporary editors.

Acknowledgments

I am pleased to acknowledge the generous financial assistance of the *Deutscher Akademischer Austauschdienst*, which enabled me to work in the Herzog August Bibliothek, Wolfenbüttel, the Deutsches Literaturarchiv, Marbach am Neckar, and in the University of Tübingen during 1983. I am also grateful to the Staff Research Fund of the University of Durham, which helped me to make extensive use of the resources of the Deutsches Volksliedarchiv and the Deutsches Sagenarchiv in Freiburg im Breisgau in 1984. I am particularly grateful for the courteous assistance I received from the staff in the latter two institutions.

Introduction

Any introduction to the movement we know as Romanticism must be prefaced with a few words of caution. There is no easy way of defining its aims, no succinct form of words with which to convey its underlying philosophy, no single common denominator to which the activities of its members can be reduced. The fact that a literary movement possesses a name does not mean that it has a uniform identity. Those who contributed to it and determined its development were individual poets and thinkers who came, equipped with their various interests and talents, from many distinct backgrounds and regions. They tended to be volatile, prone to sudden changes of heart and conversions. The movement spans a comparatively long period of time, affects all areas of artistic endeavour, and represents a turning point in the cultural life of Europe. And yet the greatest writers of the age, among them Goethe, Kleist, and Heine, were only partly committed to its ideals, but in such a way that their exact position within the Romantic pantheon remains impossible to pin down. For these and other reasons, there can be no single, pithy definition of the term Romanticism.

Most dictionaries and encyclopedias bear this out. The *Oxford Companion to English Literature* puts it bluntly: 'Romantic, a word for which, in connexion with literature, there is no generally accepted definition'. The *Oxford English Dictionary* is not much more helpful. Here Romanticism is something 'characterized. . .by, invested. . .with, romance or imaginative appeal'. Romance requires a further definition: 'Redolence or suggestion of, association with, the adventurous and chivalrous'. The *Shorter Oxford English Dictionary* is less vague and presents the product of these redolences and associations as a literature 'of a fabulous or fictitious character, having no foundation in fact, . . . fantastic, extravagant, quixotic; going beyond what is rational or practical'. Wahrig's *Deutsches Wörterbuch* assigns dates to the phenomenon: 'Die geistigen und Gefühlskräfte betonende künstlerisch-philosophische Bewegung in Europa, besonders in Deutschland zwischen 1794 und etwa 1830'. Like the other definitions, this, too, raises new problems: how does 'Geist' relate to 'Gefühl'; why the emphasis on Germany; why the exclusion of material originating before and after these dates?

One of the sources of confusion is that the word enjoys extensive currency in a debased, popular sense. 'What a romantic evening that was' or 'He certainly is the romantic type' are typical phrases that

[3]

conjure up a picture of soft music, dimmed lights, and gently refulgent erotic nostalgia. The importance of distinguishing between 'Romanticism' and 'romanticism' has frequently been stressed, but our preconceived notions about what constitutes romantic feeling in general are liable to colour our understanding of Romanticism as a literary period. Maybe it is no coincidence that the term itself is fundamentally ambiguous. How this ambiguity came about is illustrated by the origins of the word.

The root is evidently Latin *romanus*, a Roman. This points in the direction of classical antiquity — surprisingly, because if there is one thing the experts used to agree upon, it is that Romanticism and Classicism are antithetical in their aims and methods. The key to the paradox is that the word changed its meaning over the years: 'Roman' came to mean 'a citizen of the Roman empire', 'a speaker of vulgar Latin', 'a provincial' (as opposed to *latinus*). Eventually it was applied to literature written in local dialects rather than in Latin, and from here it was but a short step to 'stories told for entertainment rather than for instruction'. The medieval 'romance', the Arthurian epics and courtly lays, were 'romantic' in two senses: they originated in the old provinces of the Roman Empire (France, Britain, Spain), and they were works of the imagination. By the eighteenth century, the term had come to be applied to landscape paintings featuring idyllic, threatening, or exotic natural scenery, in which the human element, if present, was of secondary importance. 'Romantic' was the visionary, the fantastic, and the antithesis to the Classical. In painting, the Classicist would choose a temple, a palace, or a city bustling with active life as his subject; the Romantic might, by contrast, opt for a wild, stormy landscape, a jagged mountain, a ruined building or the irregular outlines of a medieval fortress. To such minds, the unfinished and disfigured elements of their surroundings proved more attractive than scenes depicting a harmony which was all too often lacking in life as they knew it. Instead of idealising classical antiquity, the Romantic looked towards the medieval period for inspiration, for it was during the medieval period that northern Europe was beset by problems that were still familiar during the eighteenth and nineteenth centuries: epidemics and war, religious upheavals, the quest for ultimate spiritual truths. Unlike Greek and Roman antiquity, the medieval world was, it seemed, governed by irrational powers. Vast fortresses were built — and allowed to disintegrate almost immediately. Immense churches and cathedrals sprang up, while the people lived in miserable hovels. Great wars, such as the

Crusades, were fought to little or no avail. Pestilences repeatedly swept across the continent and decimated its population. A new form of love was invented, 'courtly' love, the object of which was not satisfaction (as it had been for the Greeks and Romans) but, perversely, the intensification of desire, the pursuit of the impossible.

This nostalgia for all things medieval brings us close to an understanding of Romanticism as a cultural phenomenon. The principal factor is an attitude of mind that rejects what is conventional, stable, harmonious and familiar in favour of irregularity, ambiguity, and a predisposition towards the mysterious and the exotic. Nor is it difficult to see how this should have come about. It is often argued that the Romantics were rebelling against the powerful influence of neo–Classicism, which they saw as having had a stranglehold on the arts for much of the eighteenth century. French Classical drama (publicised in Germany by Gottsched), neo–Classicism in art and architecture, and the predominantly rational and optimistic philosophies of Bayle and Diderot, of Leibniz and Wolff, were equally repugnant to them. Thus the Romantics took it upon themselves to question the theories and assumptions on which earlier generations had relied. Marxist historians would probably argue that they were reacting against the lack of political and social freedom at the time and seeking refuge in the world of fantasy as a defence mechanism against despotism and a distraction from their own political impotence. Ultimately though, there is less of a difference between Classicism and Romanticism than is commonly assumed, since both involve a degree of imaginative idealisation and are in opposition not so much to one another as to Realism.

And yet Romanticism is the expression of a new attitude of mind and the product of a specific view of history not shared by previous generations. The cult of the imperfect and the fragment is with us still. It reflects the irruption of a strongly subjective element into what had previously been perceived as an ordered and harmonious universe. The medieval castle, the ruined temple, the shipwreck, are part of a conscious attempt to make a statement about time; the Romantic is more aware of history than his neo–Classical counterpart. Neo–Classical art, in its continuing imitation of ancient paradigms, claims to be timeless. It is committed to restoring what would otherwise decay and thus provides a beautiful but artificial bridge between the epochs. It assumes that human nature does not change and that moral laws hold good for all time. The implications for literature are that the Classicist conforms to tradition, uses the established metres, and observes the

[5]

constraints imposed by *genres* such as tragedy or comedy; he eschews experimentation, such as free verse, and avoids highly personal or overtly symbolic material. The Romantics were, by contrast, more willing to acknowledge the frailty of human nature, the relativity of our moral values, and the erosion of our ideals and achievements by the passage of time. An unfinished novel, a disjointed aphorism or an obscure symbolic poem is an expression of a typically Romantic awareness of man's impermanence. The conclusion to be drawn from the informality of so many Romantic artefacts is that modern man sees himself as unable to attain the high-flown moral and aesthetic ideals promulgated in the past.

It must be admitted that such generalisations are at best only half true. Any tabulation in which the 'flexibility' of Romantic art is contrasted with the 'rigidity' of Classicism, or the 'serenity' of the latter with the 'problematical nature' of the former would not apply across the board. These definitions are worth keeping in the back of one's mind, but they do not tell the whole story. Eichendorff's poetry is conventional and shows little sign of a willingness to experiment; Goethe, though in some ways a declared enemy of the Romantic movement, displays a high degree of subjectivism and versatility. Great artists will always transcend categories. To win acknowledgment, every painting, poem, or drama must offer something new and elicit a fresh emotional response. So the Romantics were by definition on the winning side. They could claim that all true poetry was Romantic poetry, which is precisely what Friedrich Schlegel did in his description of the new type of *progressive Universalpoesie*:

Die romantische Poesie ist eine progressive Universalpoesie. . . . Sie will und soll auch Poesie und Prosa, Genialität und Kritik, Kunstpoesie und Naturpoesie bald mischen, bald verschmelzen, die Poesie lebendig und gesellig und das Leben und die Gesellschaft poetisch machen, den Witz poetisieren und die Formen der Kunst mit gediegenem Bildungsstoff jeder Art anfüllen und sättigen und durch die Schwingungen des Humors beseelen. Sie umfaßt alles, was nur poetisch ist, vom größten wieder mehrere Systeme in sich enthaltenden System der Kunst bis zum Seufzer, dem Kuß, den das dichtende Kind aushaucht in kunstlosen Gesang. . . . Andere Dichtarten sind fertig und können nun vollständig zergliedert werden. Die romantische Dichtart ist noch im Werden; ja das ist ihr eigentliches Wesen, daß sie ewig nur werden, nie vollendet sein kann. Sie kann durch keine Theorie erschöpft werden. . . . (*Athenäums-Fragmente*, 1797)

We are back where we began: the leading authorities themselves claim that the term 'Romanticism' can mean more or less what they want it to. It is the works themselves that define the movement, and since there is little space in this essay for a discussion of the major literary texts, a few key words and representative examples will have to suffice. The themes to which adherents of the movement in Germany tended to return were: (1) man's limitations in a world he was ill equipped to understand, the powerlessness of reason and the supremacy of fate (Tieck, *Der blonde Eckbert*); (2) the outsider, the wanderer, the voluntary exile from society (Eichendorff, *Aus dem Leben eines Taugenichts*); (3) the criminal, the madman, the rebel (Arnim, *Der tolle Invalide auf dem Fort Ratonneau*; Kleist, *Michael Kohlhaas*); (4) the uncanny and the supernatural (Hoffmann, *Der goldene Topf*); (5) religious mysticism (Novalis, *Geistliche Lieder*, *Hymnen an die Nacht*).

If Romanticism originated as an attempt to stem the tide of rationalism, there can be no doubt that the movement derived some of its impetus from the Christian religion. The early Romantics sought to relate life to mysterious, incomprehensible forces, denying the supremacy of reason and contending that man would never be the master of his own destiny. Hence their nostalgia for the medieval period, their acute awareness of man's limitations, and the emphasis they place on the passage of time. Hence, too, the importance which figures derived from religious tradition assume in Romantic art: the hermit, the wandering pilgrim, the Virgin Mary. If Goethe and Schiller avoided committing themselves to narrow religious dogmas, the majority of the German Romantics not only accepted Christianity in one form or another, but allowed themselves to be transported to extremes of religious fervour, either in their private meditations or within the framework of organised sectarian movements and creeds such as Pietism and Roman Catholicism.

Pietism had a tremendous following in eighteenth-century Germany. The word itself is an umbrella term for many different groups of Protestant fraternities devoted to communal meditation, to close reading of the Bible, and to a strong involvement in community life. Its appeal lay both in its opposition to rationalism and pragmatism and in its antagonism to organised religion in the form of established churches and official orthodoxy. The Pietists could claim that they were returning to the essentials of the faith by stressing the importance of the individual: they were working towards the experience of rebirth on a personal level. Faith was kept alive not in the institutions that claimed to be the guardians of Christianity, and still less in their figureheads, but in each individual member of the laity. Obviously, their anti-authoritarian stance had political implications as well. The founder of the movement was Philipp Jacob Spener (1635–1705), whose pamphlet *Pia Desideria oder Herzliches Verlangen nach gottgefälliger Besserung der wahren evangelischen Kirchen* gave voice to a rousing plea for reform in 1675. Since there was little in his programme that ran counter to the interests of the state, the activities of the early Pietists were encouraged in Prussia: they helped to establish schools, encouraged the cultivation of language and literacy, performed valuable work within society, and thus assisted the reconstruction of areas devastated during the Thirty Years' War. A more militant note was struck by Nikolaus Graf von Zinzendorf (1700–60), who established the most influential Pietist community, the Herrnhuter Brüdergemeinde in Lausitz in 1727. The declared enemy of the 'enlightened' philosophy of the day, he vilified the philosopher Christian Wolff and eventually incurred the disfavour of King Frederick II of Prussia, who charged him with spreading an 'irrationalism likely to undermine the state' and in 1740 withdrew many of the privileges previously accorded to the sect. But their loose, cellular organisation ensured their survival for the best part of a century.

Since so many of their interests centred on the spoken or written word, the Pietists played an important role in determining the literary future of Germany at a time when the arts were in abeyance. They encouraged the writing of hymns and personal confessions; Zinzendorf himself is said to have recited many of his 2000-odd hymns spontaneously at devotional meetings. The religious lyric is thus one of the few forms of indigenous poetry to have thriven in a barren age during which there were no novels and most dramas were translations from the French or derivative works based on foreign models. It was chiefly in poetry that the German writers could look back to older traditions that bore comparison with those of foreign countries, and they derived some inspiration from the Baroque poets of the seventeenth century and from the language of the late medieval mystics.

This is one reason why German Romanticism is more closely bound up with Christianity than Romanticism was in other parts of Europe. Religion remained a burning issue in the German-speaking states, which were divided more or less evenly between Catholics and Protestants and had seen devastating sectarian wars in the sixteenth and seventeenth centuries. Mutual distrust and prejudice sharpened the differences between the two Christian denominations, and this may have led to conversions and near-hysteria among some of the early Romantics; there were also attempts to synthesise what was best in the two creeds, such as one finds in Novalis's *Die Christenheit oder Europa*. What we may nowadays think of as the inwardness or other-worldliness of the early Romantics is a result of their heavy dependence on a poetic vocabulary that had been handed down to them by the Baroque and Pietist poets who were their literary predecessors.

Philosophy and religion played their part in shaping the Romantic mentality. Its cornerstones were a recognition of human impermanence and a longing for stability as represented by the simple values of the past and as promised to the believer in Holy Writ. But it would be naive to assume that the phenomenon should be explained solely in terms of people's dissatisfaction with Enlightenment teachings. Inevitably, it had roots in political circumstances as well; poetry is rarely, if ever, expression of a personality in complete isolation from social factors. The most important such event for the late eighteenth century was the American War of Independence, which had shown an incredulous world that it was possible for a group of dedicated ordinary citizens to shake off an intolerable political system. A few years later, there was a Revolution in France that was directly inspired by events across the Atlantic. Wars of liberation followed elsewhere, in Greece and in other parts of the Balkans. Upheavals of this type demonstrated that the underling, the oppressed peasant and the unfranchised artisan, could exert an influence on the course of history. Romanticism was not least a democratic movement, in which more attention was paid to the literary tastes and traditions of the common people than had ever been evinced by the Classicists. Folk songs were collected and published; the impact of the most famous of these anthologies, Arnim's and Brentano's *Des Knaben Wunderhorn*, can hardly be over-emphasised. Poets such as Chamisso and Uhland spoke out on behalf of the unheard masses. Heine enthused about Napoleon, satirised the self-satisfied middle classes, and eventually turned his back on Germany. When the political tide turned and new forms of despotism established themselves in the wake of the Napoleonic Wars, Romanticism provided a ready-made vehicle for unfulfilled yearnings for greater freedom and equality. Even the most placidly disposed and conservatively minded poets could, like Eichendorff, express dissatisfaction with the present by ignoring it altogether and retreating into an inner realm of fantasy.

It could therefore be argued that while seeming to be sublimely

[9]

unaware of the social realities of the present, the Romantics were, in fact, the opposite. By dwelling on the fantastic, the remote past, by nurturing vague, unspecific longings, they were deprecating the inadequacies of the present. They used their imagination as a retreat from a world they saw as imperfect, unjust and unpoetic. The German Romantics were in a particularly unfavourable position. Most of them enjoyed less freedom than they would have done had they lived in France or England, and there was no cultural centre comparable to Paris or London towards which they could gravitate. Their social standing was not high; to be a poet was, by definition, to be an outsider. With very few exceptions, they felt that they were ostracised. This feeling of alienation affected the great men of the age in different ways: some put their faith in bizarre, quasi-religious cults (Novalis), others turned to Catholicism for consolation (Friedrich Schlegel, Brentano). Kleist committed suicide. August Schlegel and Friedrich Rückert became Orientalists. Chamisso sailed round the world, Heine escaped to Paris, Lenau, less successfully, to America. Eichendorff buried himself in an ill-paid desk job. Few of them received public recognition; Uhland was actually described by his sovereign as a useless parasite. And yet these men were responsible for a revolution in poetry comparable in its importance to the political revolutions of their time. It was they who began the gradual abandoning of traditional prosody, of rhyme, metre, Classical elegance of form and sublimity of content — a development that was to mark the beginning of literary modernism. The obscurity, the symbolism, the informality of modern verse can be traced back to their work in the early years of the nineteenth century. They were closer to the people than Goethe, Schiller, or Hölderlin had been, and they benefited from another circumstance that helped to popularise their lyrical output: their short, informal but sonorous poems lent themselves admirably to musical settings. Just as the majority of folk songs were sung, the poems of the Romantics were conceived of as *Lieder* and written with present or future composers in mind; some of their authors could, like Brentano, supply the melodies to go with their texts. So great was the interest evinced in these musical compositions that many poems have survived as poems more by virtue of the composer's efforts than by the versifier's. Thus Wilhelm Müller is remembered, if at all, as the author of Schubert's *Lieder*, and even Eichendorff would hardly be as well-known as he is today, were it not for the attention his work received during the nineteenth century from generations of composers. Some Romantic verse was set to music more than one hundred times. So intense was the enthusiasm for music in Germany during the early nineteenth century that Balzac could remark, 'Les Allemands, s'ils ne savent pas jouer des grands instruments de la Liberté, savent jouer naturellement de tous les instruments de musique', suggesting that a direct link existed between musical preoccupations and political immaturity.

There can, in fact, be little doubt that the lofty ethos of the Romantic movement was watered down by later generations. The Prussian Government soon found it expedient to encourage an interest in folk songs for narrowly patriotic reasons; as one minister, Raumer, put it, Prussian schoolchildren were to aim 'eine möglichst reiche Anzahl guter Volkslieder, wobei besonders die Vaterlandslieder zu berücksichtigen sind, einstimmig, richtig und fertig singen [zu] können'. In 1893, Bismarck himself described German song as 'an ally in war' ('Kriegsverbündeter'). The National Socialists made use of the folk song to foster a spirit of *camaraderie* and national unity, 'daß *ein* Ton alle verbinde' (*Lehrplanentwurf für Musik der Hauptschule*, 1942). Sixteenth-century broadsheets provided the models for a number of powerful *Kampflieder*, such as 'Wir sind des Geyers schwarze Haufen'. And in the postwar period, the German Democratic Republic has used traditional tunes and themes for propagandist purposes. A volume of *Lieder der Partei* published in Leipzig in 1961 includes a poem 'Die Partei, die Partei, die hat immer recht', to be sung to the tune of 'Muß i denn, muß i denn, zum Städtle hinaus'.

Whether as a vehicle of propaganda or of satire, as a source of rhetorical pathos or as a hackneyed advertising gimmick, the language of the Romantic movement continues to play its part in the evolution of the contemporary German idiom. To embark on a discussion of the influence the movement has had in these spheres would inevitably go beyond the scope of these introductory comments, which are intended to convey an initial impression of the formative influences behind Romanticism rather than to provide an exhaustive analysis. The aims of the present anthology will have been achieved if the reader arrives at a position from which to appreciate the lasting legacy of the Romantic movement in the German-speaking nations.

Introductory Reading

Hans Steffen (ed.), *Die deutsche Romantik. Poetik, Formen und Motive*, Göttingen, 1967.

Lilian R. Furst, *Romanticism*, London, 1969; 2nd ed., 1976.

— (ed.), *European Romanticism. Self-Definition*, London, 1980.

Siegbert Prawer (ed.), *The Romantic Period in Germany*, London, 1970.

Ronald Taylor (ed.), *The Romantic Tradition in Germany. An Anthology*, London, 1970.

Glyn Tegai Hughes, *Romantic German Literature*, London, 1979.

Alan Menhennet, *The Romantic Movement*, London, 1981.

Novalis
(1772–1801)

The portrait of Novalis on the previous page is taken from a copper-plate engraving of 1845, based on a portrait by an unknown artist.

Klagen eines Jünglings

Nimmer schwanden undankbar die Freuden
traumgleich mir in öde Fernen hin;
Jede färbte, lieblicher im Scheiden,
mit Erinnrung meinen trunknen Sinn;
Mit Erinnrung, die, statt zu ermüden,   5
neue, heilge Wonne mir entschloß,
und mir süßen jugendlichen Frieden
um die rebengrünen Schläfe goß.

Seit ich mehr aus schöner Wangen Röte
mehr aus sanften, blauen Augen las,   10
oft, wenn schon die scharfe Nachtluft wehte
im beseeltern Traume mich vergaß;
meinem Herzen nachbarlicher, wärmer,
da den Schlag der Nachtigall empfand,
und entfernt von meinem Klärchen ärmer   15
mich als jeder dürft'ge Pilger fand:

Lachet, ew'ge Gottheit in dem Blicke,
mich mein sonnenschönes Leben an,
Amor täuscht mich nicht mit List und Tücke,
Ganymeda nicht mit kurzem Wahn;   20
Jedes Lüftchen nähert sich mir milder,
das dort Blüten wild herunter haucht;
üppig drängen immer frische Bilder
sich zu mir, in Rosenöl getaucht.

Zypris Tauben warten schon mit Kränzen   25
und mit Traubenbechern meiner dort,
und in leichtverschlungnen Freudentänzen
reißet Amors Bruderschwarm mich fort.
Von der Grazien und Musen Lippen
schmachtet mir entgegen mancher Kuß;   30
Götterwonne kann ich selig nippen,
schwelgen da im freundlichsten Genuß.

[15]

Dennoch lodern öfters Purpurgluten
Mir um meine Wang und meine Stirn,
wenn sich unter Stürmen, unter Fluten,   35
wie des Abends leuchtendes Gestirn,
mir, umstrahlt von echter Freiheit Kranze,
eines edlen Dulders Seele zeigt,
den der Himmel nicht in seinem Glanze
nicht die Höll' in ihren Nächten beugt.   40

Kraftlos fühl' ich mich von dem Geschicke
zum unmännlichern Genuß verdammt;
vor Gefahren beb' ich feig zurücke
weil nicht Mut in meinem Busen flammt.
Weibisch hat das Schicksal mich erzogen,   45
nicht sein Liebling, nur sein Sklav bin ich;
Amor hat mich schmeichlerisch umflogen
statt der Sorge, die mir stets entwich.

Statt der ernstern, rühmlicheren Lanze
wieget einen Hirtenstab mein Arm;   50
nimmer wurde mir im Waffentanze
aber oft im bunten Reigen warm:
alle großen, strahlenden Gefahren
Hat mein Schicksal von mir abgewandt,
und nur unter frohe Mädchenscharen   55
statt in Feindes Haufen mich gesandt.

Parze, hast du jemals deine Spindel
nach dem Flehn des Erdensohns gedreht,
dem kein bald entwichner Zauberschwindel
um die flammendheißen Schläfe weht: 60
O! so nimm, was Tausende begehrten,
was mir üppig deine Milde lieh,
gib mir Sorgen, Elend und Beschwerden,
und dafür dem Geiste Energie.

Ungeduldig soll die Flamme lodern   65
meines Dankes dann von dem Altar;
nichts mehr sollen meine Wünsche fordern,
frei und gnügsam macht mich die Gefahr;
Doch versagest du mir diese Bitte
O! so kürze, wenn du streng nicht bist,
mindestens geschwind nur meine Schritte:
nimm dies Leben, das nicht Leben ist.

* * * * *

Wer einsam sitzt in seiner Kammer,
Und schwere, bittre Tränen weint,
Wem nur gefärbt von Not und Jammer
Die Nachbarschaft umher erscheint;

Wer in das Bild vergangner Zeiten   5
Wie tief in einen Abgrund sieht,
In welchen ihn von allen Seiten
Ein süßes Weh hinunter zieht; —

Es ist, als lägen Wunderschätze
Da unten für ihn aufgehäuft,   10
Nach deren Schloß in wilder Hetze
Mit atemloser Brust er greift.

Die Zukunft liegt in öder Dürre
Entsetzlich lang und bang vor ihm —
Er schweift umher, allein und irre,   15
Und sucht sich selbst mit Ungestüm.

Ich fall' ihm weinend in die Arme:
Auch mir war einst, wie dir, zumut,
Doch ich genas von meinem Harme,
Und weiß nun, wo man ewig ruht.   20

Dich muß, wie mich, ein Wesen trösten,
Das innig liebte, litt und starb;
Das selbst für die, die ihm am wehsten
Getan, mit tausend Freuden starb.

Er starb, und dennoch alle Tage   25
Vernimmst du seine Lieb' und ihn,
Und kannst getrost in jeder Lage
Ihn zärtlich in die Arme ziehn.

Mit ihm kommt neues Blut und Leben
In dein erstorbenes Gebein —   30
Und wenn du ihm dein Herz gegeben,
So ist auch seines ewig dein.

Was du verlorst, hat er gefunden;
Du triffst bei ihm, was du geliebt:
Und ewig bleibt mit dir verbunden,   35
Was seine Hand dir wiedergibt.

* * * * *

Ich sehe dich in tausend Bildern,
Maria, lieblich ausgedrückt,
Doch keins von allen kann dich schildern,
Wie meine Seele dich erblickt.

Ich weiß nur, daß der Welt Getümmel   5
Seitdem mir wie ein Traum verweht,
Und ein unnennbar süßer Himmel
Mir ewig im Gemüte steht.

* * * * *

[18]

(Das Lied des Einsiedlers)

Gern verweil ich noch im Tale
Lächelnd in der tiefen Nacht,
Denn der Liebe volle Schale
Wird mir täglich dargebracht.

Ihre heilgen Tropfen heben   5
Meine Seele hoch empor,
Und ich steh in diesem Leben
Trunken an des Himmels Tor.

Eingewiegt in selges Schauen
Ängstigt mein Gemüt kein Schmerz.   10
O! die Königin der Frauen
Gibt mir ihr getreues Herz.

Bangverweinte Jahre haben
Diesen schlechten Ton verklärt,
Und ein Bild ihm eingegraben,   15
Das ihm Ewigkeit gewährt.

Jene lange Zahl von Tagen
Dünkt mir nur ein Augenblick;
Werd ich einst von hier getragen
Schau ich dankbar noch zurück.   20

*   *   *   *   *

[19]

Wenn nicht mehr Zahlen und Figuren
Sind Schlüssel aller Kreaturen,
Wenn die, so singen oder küssen,
Mehr als die Tiefgelehrten wissen,
Wenn sich die Welt ins freie Leben,   5
Und in die Welt wird zurück begeben,
Wenn dann sich wieder Licht und Schatten
Zu echter Klarheit werden gatten,
Und man in Märchen und Gedichten
Erkennt die ewgen Weltgeschichten,   10
Dann fliegt vor Einem geheimen Wort
Das ganze verkehrte Wesen sofort.

* * * * *

(Das Lied der Toten)

Lobt doch unsre stillen Feste,
Unsre Gärten, unsre Zimmer,
Das bequeme Hausgeräte,
Unser Hab und Gut.
Täglich kommen neue Gäste,   5
Diese früh, die andern späte,
Auf den weiten Herden immer
Lodert frische Lebens-Glut.

Tausend zierliche Gefäße
Einst betaut mit tausend Tränen,   10
Goldne Ringe, Sporen, Schwerter,
Sind in unserm Schatz:
Viel Kleinodien und Juwelen
Wissen wir in dunkeln Höhlen,
Keiner kann den Reichtum zählen,   15
Zählt' er auch ohn' Unterlaß.

Kinder der Vergangenheiten,
Helden aus den grauen Zeiten,
Der Gestirne Riesengeister,
Wunderlich gesellt,   20
Holde Frauen, ernste Meister,
Kinder und verlebte Greise
Sitzen hier in Einem Kreise,
Wohnen in der alten Welt.

Keiner wird sich je beschweren,   25
Keiner wünschen fort zu gehen,
Wer an unsern vollen Tischen
Einmal fröhlich saß.
Klagen sind nicht mehr zu hören,
Keine Wunden mehr zu sehen,   30
Keine Tränen abzuwischen;
Ewig läuft das Stundenglas.

Tiefgerührt von heilger Güte
Und versenkt in selges Schauen
Steht der Himmel im Gemüte,   35
Wolkenloses Blau;
Lange fliegende Gewande
Tragen uns durch Frühlingsauen,
Und es weht in diesem Lande
Nie ein Lüftchen kalt und rauh.   40

Süßer Reiz der Mitternächte,
Stiller Kreis geheimer Mächte,
Wollust rätselhafter Spiele,
Wir nur kennen euch.
Wir nur sind am hohen Ziele,   45
Bald in Strom uns zu ergießen
Dann in Tropfen zu zerfließen
Und zu nippen auch zugleich.

Uns ward erst die Liebe, Leben;
Innig wie die Elemente   50
Mischen wir des Daseins Fluten,
Brausend Herz mit Herz.
Lüstern scheiden sich die Fluten,
Denn der Kampf der Elemente
Ist der Liebe höchstes Leben,   55
Und des Herzens eignes Herz.

Leiser Wünsche süßes Plaudern
Hören wir allein, und schauen
Immerdar in selge Augen,
Schmecken nichts als Mund und Kuß.   60
Alles was wir nur berühren
Wird zu heißen Balsamfrüchten,
Wird zu weichen zarten Brüsten,
Opfer kühner Lust.

Immer wächst und blüht Verlangen   65
Am Geliebten festzuhangen,
Ihn im Innern zu empfangen,
Eins mit ihm zu sein,
Seinem Durste nicht zu wehren,
Sich im Wechsel zu verzehren,   70
Von einander sich zu nähren,
Von einander nur allein.

So in Lieb' und hoher Wollust
Sind wir immerdar versunken,
Seit der wilde trübe Funken   75
Jener Welt erlosch;
Seit der Hügel sich geschlossen,
Und der Scheiterhaufen sprühte,
Und dem schauernden Gemüte
Nun das Erdgesicht zerfloß.   80

[22]

Zauber der Erinnerungen,
Heilger Wehmut süße Schauer
Haben innig uns durchklungen,
Kühlen unsre Glut.
Wunden gibt's, die ewig schmerzen, 85
Eine göttlich tiefe Trauer
Wohnt in unser aller Herzen,
Löst uns auf in Eine Flut.

Und in dieser Flut ergießen
Wir uns auf geheime Weise 90
In den Ozean des Lebens
Tief in Gott hinein;
Und aus seinem Herzen fließen
Wir zurück zu unserm Kreise,
Und der Geist des höchsten Strebens 95
Taucht in unsre Wirbel ein.

Schüttelt eure goldnen Ketten
Mit Smaragden und Rubinen,
Und die blanken saubern Spangen,
Blitz und Klang zugleich. 100
Aus des feuchten Abgrunds Betten,
Aus den Gräbern und Ruinen,
Himmelsrosen auf den Wangen
Schwebt ins bunte Fabelreich.

Könnten doch die Menschen wissen, 105
Unsre künftigen Genossen,
Daß bei allen ihren Freuden
Wir geschäftig sind:
Jauchzend würden sie verscheiden,
Gern das bleiche Dasein missen, — 110
O! die Zeit ist bald verflossen,
Kommt Geliebte doch geschwind!

Helft uns nur den Erdgeist binden,
Lernt den Sinn des Todes fassen
Und das Wort des Lebens finden; 115
Einmal kehrt euch um.
Deine Macht muß bald verschwinden,
Dein erborgtes Licht verblassen,
Werden dich in kurzem binden,
Erdgeist, deine Zeit ist um. 120

Clemens Brentano
(1778–1842)

The portrait of Brentano on the previous page is taken from a drawing by Wilhelm von Schadow (1805).

Lore Lay

Zu Bacharach am Rheine
Wohnt' eine Zauberin,
Sie war so schön und feine
Und riß viel Herzen hin.

Und brachte viel zu Schanden   5
Der Männer rings umher;
Aus ihren Liebesbanden
War keine Rettung mehr.

Der Bischof ließ sie laden
Vor geistliche Gewalt —   10
Und mußte sie begnaden,
So schön war ihr' Gestalt.

Er sprach zu ihr gerühret:
»Du arme Lore Lay!
Wer hat dich denn verführet   15
Zu böser Zauberei?«

»Herr Bischof, laßt mich sterben,
Ich bin des Lebens müd,
Weil jeder muß verderben,
Der meine Augen sieht.   20

Die Augen sind zwei Flammen,
Mein Arm ein Zauberstab —
O legt mich in die Flammen!
O brechet mir den Stab!«

»Ich kann dich nicht verdammen,   25
Bis du mir erst bekennt,
Warum in diesen Flammen
Mein eigen Herz schon brennt.

Den Stab kann ich nicht brechen,
Du schöne Lore Lay!   30
Ich müßte dann zerbrechen
Mein eigen Herz entzwei."

„Herr Bischof, mit mir Armen
Treibt nicht so bösen Spott,
Und bittet um Erbarmen   35
Für mich den lieben Gott.

Ich darf nicht länger leben,
Ich liebe keinen mehr —
Den Tod sollt Ihr mir geben,
Drum kam ich zu Euch her. —   40

Mein Schatz hat mich betrogen,
Hat sich von mir gewandt,
Ist fort von hier gezogen,
Fort in ein fremdes Land.

Die Augen sanft und wilde,   45
Die Wangen rot und weiß,
Die Worte still und milde
Das ist mein Zauberkreis.

Ich selbst muß drin verderben,
Das Herz tut mir so weh,   50
Vor Schmerzen möcht ich sterben,
Wenn ich mein Bildnis seh.

Drum laßt mein Recht mich finden,
Mich sterben, wie ein Christ,
Denn alles muß verschwinden,   55
Weil er nicht bei mir ist."

Drei Ritter läßt er holen:
„Bringt sie ins Kloster hin,
Geh Lore! — Gott befohlen
Sei dein berückter Sinn.   60

Du sollst ein Nönnchen werden,
Ein Nönnchen schwarz und weiß,
Bereite dich auf Erden
Zu deines Todes Reis'."

Zum Kloster sie nun ritten,   65
Die Ritter alle drei,
Und traurig in der Mitten
Die schöne Lore Lay.

„O Ritter, laßt mich gehen
Auf diesen Felsen groß,   70
Ich will noch einmal sehen
Nach meines Lieben Schloß.

Ich will noch einmal sehen
Wohl in den tiefen Rhein,
Und dann ins Kloster gehen   75
Und Gottes Jungfrau sein."

Der Felsen ist so jähe,
So steil ist seine Wand,
Doch klimmt sie in die Höhe,
Bis daß sie oben stand.   80

Es binden die drei Ritter
Die Rosse unten an,
Und klettern immer weiter
Zum Felsen auch hinan.

Die Jungfrau sprach: „Da gehet   85
Ein Schifflein auf dem Rhein,
Der in dem Schifflein stehet,
Der soll mein Liebster sein.

Mein Herz wird mir so munter,
Er muß mein Liebster sein!" —   90
Da lehnt sie sich hinunter
Und stürzet in den Rhein.

[29]

Die Ritter mußten sterben,
Sie konnten nicht hinab,
Sie mußten all verderben   95
Ohn Priester und ohn Grab.

Wer hat dies Lied gesungen?
Ein Schiffer auf dem Rhein,
Und immer hats geklungen
Von dem Dreiritterstein: 100

Lore Lay
Lore Lay
Lore Lay

Als wären es meiner drei.

* * * * *

Großmutter Schlangenköchin

Maria, wo bist du zur Stube gewesen?
Maria, mein einziges Kind!

Ich bin bei meiner Großmutter gewesen,
Ach weh! Frau Mutter, wie weh!

Was hat sie dir dann zu essen gegeben?   5
Maria, mein einziges Kind!

Sie hat mir gebackne Fischlein gegeben,
Ach weh! Frau Mutter, wie weh!

Wo hat sie dir dann das Fischlein gefangen?
Maria, mein einziges Kind!   10

Sie hat es in ihrem Krautgärtlein gefangen,
Ach weh! Frau Mutter, wie weh!

Womit hat sie dann das Fischlein gefangen?
Maria, mein einziges Kind!

Sie hat es mit Stecken und Ruten gefangen,   15
Ach weh! Frau Mutter, wie weh!

Wo ist dann das übrige vom Fischlein hinkommen?
Maria, mein einziges Kind!

Sie hat's ihrem schwarzbraunen Hündlein gegeben,
Ach weh! Frau Mutter, wie weh!   20

Wo ist dann das schwarzbraune Hündlein hinkommen?
Maria, mein einziges Kind!

Es ist in tausend Stücke zersprungen,
Ach weh! Frau Mutter, wie weh!

Maria, wo soll ich dein Bettlein hin machen?   25
Maria, mein einziges Kind!

Du sollst mir's auf den Kirchhof machen,
Ach weh! Frau Mutter, wie weh!

* * * * *

Der Spinnerin Nachtlied

Es sang vor langen Jahren
Wohl auch die Nachtigall,
Das war wohl süßer Schall,
Da wir zusammen waren.

Ich sing und kann nicht weinen,   5
Und spinne so allein
Den Faden klar und rein
So lang der Mond wird scheinen.

[31]

Als wir zusammen waren
Da sang die Nachtigall,   10
Nun mahnet mich ihr Schall
Daß du von mir gefahren.

So oft der Mond mag scheinen,
Denk ich wohl dein allein,
Mein Herz ist klar und rein,   15
Gott wolle uns vereinen.

Seit du von mir gefahren,
Singt stets die Nachtigall,
Ich denk bei ihrem Schall,
Wie wir zusammen waren.   20

Gott wolle uns vereinen,
Hier spinn ich so allein,
Der Mond scheint klar und rein,
Ich sing und möchte weinen.

* * * * *

Die Welt war mir zuwider
Die Berge lagen auf mir
Der Himmel war mir zu nieder
Ich sehnte mich nach dir, nach dir,
O lieb Mädel, wie schlecht bist du!   5

Ich trieb wohl durch die Gassen
Zwei lange Jahre mich
An den Ecken mußt ich passen
Und harren nur auf dich, auf dich.
O lieb Mädel, wie schlecht bist du!   10

Und alle Liebeswunden
Die brachen auf in mir
Als ich dich endlich gefunden
Ich lebt' und starb in dir, in dir!
O lieb Mädel, wie schlecht bist du!   15

Ich hab vor deiner Türe
Die hellgestirnte Nacht,
Daß dich mein Lieben rühre
Oft liebeskrank durchwacht.
O lieb Mädel, wie schlecht bist du!   20

Ich ging nicht zu dem Feste
Trank nicht den edlen Wein
Ertrug den Spott der Gäste
Um nur bei dir zu sein.
O lieb Mädel, wie schlecht bist du!   25

Bin zitternd zu dir gekommen
Als wärst du ein Jungfräulein,
Hab dich in Arm genommen
Als wärst du mein allein, allein.
O lieb Mädel, wie schlecht bist du!   30

Wie schlecht du sonst gewesen
Vergaß ich liebend in mir
Und all dein elendes Wesen
Vergab ich herzlich dir, ach dir,
O lieb Mädel, wie schlecht bist du!   35

Als du mir nackt gegeben
Zur Nacht den kühlen Trank
Vergiftetest du mein Leben,
Da war meine Seele so krank, so krank,
O lieb Mädel, wie schlecht bist du!   40

Bergab bin ich gegangen
Mit dir zu jeder Stund,
Hab fest an dir gehangen
Und ging mit dir zugrund.
O lieb Mädel, wie schlecht bist du!   45

Es hat sich an der Wunde
Die Schlange fest gesaugt
Hat mit dem gift'gen Munde
Den Tod in mich gehaucht.
O lieb Mädel, wie schlecht bist du!   50

Und ach in all den Peinen
War ich nur gut und treu
Daß ich mich nannt' den Deinen
Ich nimmermehr bereu, bereu.
O lieb Mädel, wie schlecht bist du!   55

* * * * *

Frühlingsschrei eines Knechtes aus der Tiefe

Meister, ohne dein Erbarmen
Muß im Abgrund ich verzagen,
Willst du nicht mit starken Armen
Wieder mich zum Lichte tragen.

Jährlich greifet deine Güte,   5
In die Erde, in die Herzen,
Jährlich weckest du die Blüte,
Weckst in mir die alten Schmerzen.

Einmal nur zum Licht geboren,
Aber tausendmal gestorben,   10
Bin ich ohne dich verloren,
Ohne dich in mir verdorben.

[34]

Wenn sich so die Erde reget,
Wenn die Luft so sonnig wehet,
Dann wird auch die Flut beweget,   15
Die in Todesbanden stehet.

Und in meinem Herzen schauert
Ein betrübter bittrer Bronnen,
Wenn der Frühling draußen lauert,
Kömmt die Angstflut angeronnen.   20

Weh! durch gift'ge Erdenlagen,
Wie die Zeit sie angeschwemmet,
Habe ich den Schacht geschlagen,
Und er ist nur schwach verdämmet.

Wenn nun rings die Quellen schwellen,   25
Wenn der Grund gebärend ringet,
Brechen her die gift'gen Wellen,
Die kein Fluch, kein Witz mir zwinget.

Andern ruf ich: Schwimme, schwimme,
Mir kann solcher Ruf nicht taugen,   30
Denn in mir ja steigt die grimme
Sündflut, bricht aus meinen Augen.

Und dann scheinen bös Gezüchte
Mir die bunten Lämmer alle,
Die ich grüßte, süße Früchte,   35
Die mir reiften, bittre Galle.

Herr, erbarme du dich meiner,
Daß mein Herz neu blühend werde,
Mein erbarmte sich noch keiner
Von den Frühlingen der Erde.   40

Meister, wenn dir alle Hände
Nahn mit süßerfüllten Schalen,
Kann ich mit der bittern Spende
Meine Schuld dir nimmer zahlen.

Ach, wie ich auch tiefer wühle,   45
Wie ich schöpfe, wie ich weine,
Nimmer ich den Schwall erspüle
Zum Kristallgrund fest und reine.

Immer stürzen mir die Wände,
Jede Schicht hat mich belogen,   50
Und die arbeitblut'gen Hände
Brennen in den bittern Wogen.

Weh! der Raum wird immer enger,
Wilder, wüster stets die Wogen,
Herr, o Herr! ich treib's nicht länger,   55
Schlage deinen Regenbogen.

Herr, ich mahne dich, verschone,
Herr! ich hört in jungen Tagen,
Wunderbare Rettung wohne
Ach, in deinem Blute, sagen.   60

Und so muß ich zu dir schreien,
Schreien aus der bittern Tiefe,
Könntest du auch nicht verzeihen,
Daß dein Knecht so kühnlich riefe!

Daß des Lichtes Quelle wieder   65
Rein und heilig in mir flute,
Träufle einen Tropfen nieder,
Jesus, mir, von deinem Blute!

* * * * *

Wenn der lahme Weber träumt, er webe,
Träumt die kranke Lerche auch, sie schwebe,
Träumt die stumme Nachtigall, sie singe,
Daß das Herz des Widerhalls zerspringe,
Träumt das blinde Huhn, es zähl' die Kerne,   5
Und der drei je zählte kaum, die Sterne,
Träumt das starre Erz, gar linde tau' es,
Und das Eisenherz, ein Kind vertrau' es,
Träumt die taube Nüchternheit, sie lausche,
Wie der Traube Schüchternheit berausche;   10
Kömmt dann Wahrheit mutternackt gelaufen,
Führt der hellen Töne Glanzgefunkel
Und der grellen Lichter Tanz durchs Dunkel,
Rennt den Traum sie schmerzlich übern Haufen,
Horch! die Fackel lacht, horch! Schmerz-Schalmeien   15
Der erwachten Nacht ins Herz all schreien,
Weh, ohn Opfer gehn die süßen Wunder,
Gehn die armen Herzen einsam unter!

Adelbert von Chamisso
(1781–1838)

The portrait of Chamisso on the previous page is taken from an undated copperplate engraving based on a portrait by Robert Reinick.

Das Schloß Boncourt

Ich träum als Kind mich zurücke
Und schüttle mein greises Haupt;
Wie sucht ihr mich heim, ihr Bilder,
Die lang ich vergessen geglaubt?

Hoch ragt aus schatt'gen Gehegen   5
Ein schimmerndes Schloß hervor,
Ich kenne die Türme, die Zinnen,
Die steinerne Brücke, das Tor.

Es schauen vom Wappenschilde
Die Löwen so traulich mich an;   10
Ich grüße die alten Bekannten
Und eile den Burghof hinan.

Dort liegt die Sphinx am Brunnen,
Dort grünt der Feigenbaum,
Dort, hinter diesen Fenstern,   15
Verträumt ich den ersten Traum.

Ich tret in die Burgkapelle
Und suche des Ahnherrn Grab;
Dort ist's, dort hängt vom Pfeiler
Das alte Gewaffen herab.   20

Noch lesen umflort die Augen
Die Züge der Inschrift nicht,
Wie hell durch die bunten Scheiben
Das Licht darüber auch bricht.

So stehst du, o Schloß meiner Väter,   25
Mir treu und fest in dem Sinn,
Und bist von der Erde verschwunden,
Der Pflug geht über dich hin.

Sei fruchtbar, o teurer Boden,
Icht segne dich mild und gerührt,   30
Und segn' ihn zwiefach, wer immer
Den Pflug nun über dich führt.

Ich aber will auf mich raffen,
Mein Saitenspiel in der Hand,
Die Weiten der Erde durchschweifen   35
Und singen von Land zu Land.

* * * * *

Der Invalid im Irrenhaus

Leipzig, Leipzig! arger Boden,
Schmach für Unbill schafftest du.
Freiheit! hieß es, vorwärts, vorwärts!
Trankst mein rotes Blut, wozu?

Freiheit! rief ich, vorwärts, vorwärts!   5
Was ein Tor nicht alles glaubt!
Und von schwerem Säbelstreiche
Ward gespalten mir das Haupt.

Und ich lag, und abwärts wälzte
Unheilschwanger sich die Schlacht,   10
Über mich und über Leichen
Sank die kalte, finstre Nacht.

Aufgewacht zu grausen Schmerzen,
Brennt die Wunde mehr und mehr;
Und ich liege hier gebunden,   15
Grimm'ge Wächter um mich her.

Schrei ich wütend noch nach Freiheit,
Nach dem bluterkauften Glück,
Peitscht der Wächter mit der Peitsche
Mich in schnöde Ruh zurück.   20

[42]

* * * * *

Das Riesen-Spielzeug

Burg Niedeck ist im Elsaß der Sage wohlbekannt,
Die Höhe, wo vor Zeiten die Burg der Riesen stand;
Sie selbst ist nun zerfallen, die Stätte wüst und leer,
Du fragest nach den Riesen, du findest sie nicht mehr.

Einst kam das Riesen-Fräulein aus jener Burg hervor,   5
Erging sich sonder Wartung und spielend vor dem Tor,
Und stieg hinab den Abhang bis in das Tal hinein,
Neugierig zu erkunden, wie's unten möchte sein.

Mit wen'gen raschen Schritten durchkreuzte sie den Wald,
Erreichte gegen Haslach das Land der Menschen bald,   10
Und Städte dort und Dörfer und das bestellte Feld
Erschienen ihren Augen gar eine fremde Welt.

Wie jetzt zu ihren Füßen sie spähend niederschaut,
Bemerkt sie einen Bauer, der seinen Acker baut;
Es kriecht das kleine Wesen einher so sonderbar,   15
Es glitzert in der Sonne der Pflug so blank und klar.

"Ei! artig Spielding!" ruft sie, "das nehm ich mit nach
                                        Haus."
Sie knieet nieder, spreitet behend ihr Tüchlein aus,
Und feget mit den Händen, was da sich alles regt,
Zu Haufen in das Tüchlein, das sie zusammenschlägt;   20

Und eilt mit freud'gen Sprüngen — man weiß, wie Kinder
                                        sind —
Zur Burg hinan und suchet den Vater auf geschwind:
"Ei Vater, lieber Vater, ein Spielding wunderschön!
So Allerliebstes sah ich noch nie auf unsern Höhn."

Der Alte saß am Tische und trank den kühlen Wein,   25
Er schaut sie an behaglich, er fragt das Töchterlein:
"Was Zappeliges bringst du in deinem Tuch herbei?
Du hüpfest ja vor Freuden; laß sehen, was es sei."

Sie spreitet aus das Tüchlein und fängt behutsam an,
Den Bauer aufzustellen, den Pflug und das Gespann;   30
Wie alles auf dem Tische sie zierlich aufgebaut,
So klatscht sie in die Hände und springt und jubelt laut.

Der Alte wird gar ernsthaft und wiegt sein Haupt und
                                                  spricht:
"Was hast du angerichtet? das ist kein Spielzeug nicht;
Wo du es hergenommen, da trag es wieder hin!   35
Der Bauer ist kein Spielzeug, was kommt dir in den Sinn!

Sollst gleich und ohne Murren erfüllen mein Gebot;
Denn, wäre nicht der Bauer, so hättest du kein Brot;
Es sprießt der Stamm der Riesen aus Bauernmark hervor,
Der Bauer ist kein Spielzeug, da sei uns Gott davor!"   40

Burg Niedeck ist im Elsaß der Sage wohlbekannt,
Die Höhe, wo vor Zeiten die Burg der Riesen stand,
Sie selbst ist nun verfallen, die Stätte wüst und leer,
Und fragst du nach den Riesen, du findest sie nicht mehr.

* * * * *

Die Weiber von Winsperg

Der erste Hohenstaufen, der König Konrad, lag
Mit Heeresmacht vor Winsperg seit manchem langen Tag,
Der Welfe war geschlagen, noch wehrte sich das Nest,
Die unverzagten Städter, die hielten es noch fest.

Der Hunger kam, der Hunger! das ist ein scharfer Dorn,   5
Nun suchten sie die Gnade, nun trafen sie den Zorn:
"Ihr habt mir hier erschlagen gar manchen Degen wert,
Und öffnet ihr die Tore, so trifft euch doch das Schwert."

[44]

Da sind die Weiber kommen: "Und muß es also sein,
Gewährt uns freien Abzug, wir sind vom Blute rein."   10
Da hat sich vor den Armen des Helden Zorn gekühlt,
Da hat ein sanft Erbarmen im Herzen er gefühlt.

"Die Weiber mögen abziehn und jede habe frei,
Was sie vermag zu tragen und ihr das Liebste sei;
Laßt ziehn mit ihrer Bürde sie ungehindert fort,   15
Das ist des Königs Meinung, das ist des Königs Wort."

Und als der frühe Morgen im Osten kaum gegraut,
Da hat ein seltnes Schauspiel vom Lager man geschaut;
Es öffnet leise, leise sich das bedrängte Tor,
Es schwankt ein Zug von Weibern mit schwerem Schritt
                         hervor.   20

Tief beugt die Last sie nieder, die auf dem Nacken ruht,
Sie tragen ihre Eh'herrn, das ist ihr liebstes Gut.
"Halt an die argen Weiber!" ruft drohend mancher
                         Wicht; —
Der Kanzler spricht bedeutsam: "Das war die Meinung
                         nicht."

Da hat, wie er's vernommen, der fromme Herr gelacht: 25
"Und war es nicht die Meinung, sie haben's gut gemacht;
Gesprochen ist gesprochen, das Königswort besteht,
Und zwar von keinem Kanzler zerdeutelt und zerdreht."

So war das Gold der Krone wohl rein und unentweiht.
Die Sage schallt herüber aus halbvergeßner Zeit.   30
Im Jahr elfhundertvierzig, wie ich's verzeichnet fand,
Galt Königswort noch heilig im deutschen Vaterland.

* * * * *

[45]

Das Dampfroß

Schnell! schnell, mein Schmidt, mit des Rosses Beschlag!
Derweil du zauderst, verstreicht der Tag. —
„Wie dampfet dein ungeheures Pferd!
Wo eilst du so hin, mein Ritter wert?" —

Schnell! schnell, mein Schmidt! Wer die Erde umkreist   5
Von Ost in West, wie die Schule beweist,
Der kommt, das hat er von seiner Müh,
Ans Ziel um einen Tag zu früh.

Mein Dampfroß, Muster der Schnelligkeit,
Läßt hinter sich die laufende Zeit,   10
Und nimmt's zur Stunde nach Westen den Lauf,
Kommt's gestern von Osten schon wieder herauf.

Ich habe der Zeit ihr Geheimnis geraubt,
Von Gestern zu Gestern zurück sie geschraubt,
Und schraube zurück sie von Tag zu Tag,   15
Wie einst ich zu Adam gelangen mag.

Ich habe die Mutter, sonderbar!
In der Stunde besucht, da sie mich gebar,
Ich selber stand der Kreißenden bei,
Und habe vernommen mein erstes Geschrei.   20

Viel tausend Mal, der Sonne voran,
Vollbracht ich im Fluge noch meine Bahn,
Bis heut ich hier zu besuchen kam
Großvater als glücklichen Bräutigam.

Großmutter ist die lieblichste Braut,   25
Die je mit Augen ich noch erschaut;
Er aber, grämlich, zu eifern geneigt,
Hat ohne weiteres die Tür mir gezeigt.

Schnell! schnell, mein Schmidt! mich ekelt schier,
Die jetzt verläuft, die Zeit von Papier;   30
Zurück hindurch! es verlangt mich schon
Zu sehen den Kaiser Napoleon.

Ich sprech ihn zuerst auf Helena,
Den Gruß der Nachwelt bring ich ihm da;
Dann sprech ich ihn früher beim Krönungsfest,   35
Und warn ihn, — o hielt' er die Warnung fest!

Bist fertig, mein Schmidt? nimm deinen Sold,
Ein Tausend Neunhundert geprägtes Gold.
Zu Roß! Hurrah! nach Westen gejagt,
Hier wieder vorüber, wann gestern es tagt! —   40

„Mein Ritter, mein Ritter, du kommst daher,
Wohin wir gehen, erzähle noch mehr;
Du weißt, o sag es, ob fällt, ob steigt
Der Cours, der jetzt so schwankend sich zeigt?

Ein Wort, ein Wort nur im Vertraun!   45
Ist's weis, auf Rothschild Häuser zu baun?" —
Schon hatte der Reiter die Feder gedrückt,
Das Dampfroß fern ihn den Augen entrückt.

* * * * *

Pech

Wahrlich aus mir hätte vieles
Werden können in der Welt,
Hätte tückisch nicht mein Schicksal
Sich mir in den Weg gestellt.

Hoher Ruhm war zu erwerben,   5
Wenn die Waffen ich erkor;
Mich den Kugeln preis zu geben,
War ich aber nicht der Tor.

[47]

Um der Musen Gunst zu buhlen
War ich minder schon entfernt;   10
Ein Gelehrter wär ich worden,
Hätt ich lesen nur gelernt.

Bei den Frauen, sonder Zweifel,
Hätt ich noch mein Glück gemacht,
Hätten sie mich aller Orten   15
Nicht unmenschlich ausgelacht.

Wie zum reichen Mann geboren,
Hätt ich diesen Stand erwählt,
Hätte nicht vor allen Dingen
Immer mir das Geld gefehlt.   20

Über einen Staat zu herrschen,
War vor allen ich der Mann,
Meine Gaben und Talente
Wiesen diesen Platz mir an.

König hätt ich werden sollen,   25
Wo man über Fürsten klagt.
Doch mein Vater war ein Bürger,
Und das ist genug gesagt.

Wahrlich aus mir hätte vieles
Werden können in der Welt,   30
Hätte tückisch nicht mein Schicksal
Sich mir in den Weg gestellt.

Des Knaben Wunderhorn

Alte deutsche Lieder

Achim v. Arnim. Clemens Brentano.

— · —

Heidelberg. bey Mohr u. Zimmer.
Frankfurt bey J. C. B. Mohr.
1806.

The title-page of *Das Knaben Wunderhorn* reproduced on the previous page is that of the first edition (1806).

Der Rattenfänger von Hameln

Wer ist der bunte Mann im Bilde?
Er führet Böses wohl im Schilde,
Er pfeift so wild und so bedacht;
Ich hätt mein Kind ihm nicht gebracht!

In Hameln fochten Mäus und Ratzen   5
Bei hellem Tage mit den Katzen,
Es war viel Not; der Rat bedacht,
Wie andre Kunst zuweggebracht.

Da fand sich ein der Wundermann,
Mit bunten Kleidern angetan,   10
Pfiff Ratz und Mäus zusamm' ohn Zahl,
Ersäuft sie in der Weser all.

Der Rat will ihm dafür nicht geben,
Was ihm ward zugesagt soeben;
Sie meinten, das ging gar zu leicht   15
Und wär wohl gar ein Teufelsstreich.

Wie hart er auch den Rat besprochen,
Sie dräuten seinem bösen Pochen,
Er konnt' zuletzt vor der Gemein
Nur auf dem Dorfe sicher sein.   20

Die Stadt, von solcher Not befreit,
Im großen Dankfest sich erfreuet,
Im Betstuhl saßen alle Leut,
Es läuten alle Glocken weit.

Die Kinder spielten in den Gassen,   25
Der Wundermann durchzog die Straßen,
Er kam und pfiff zusamm' geschwind
Wohl auf ein hundert schöne Kind.

Der Hirt sah sie zur Weser gehen,
Und keiner hat sie je gesehen, 30
Verloren sind sie an dem Tag
Zu ihrer Eltern Weh und Klag.

Im Strome schweben Irrlicht nieder,
Die Kindlein frischen drin die Glieder,
Dann pfeifet er sie wieder ein, 35
Für seine Kunst bezahlt zu sein.

Ihr Leute, wenn ihr Gift wollt legen,
So hütet doch die Kinder gegen,
Das Gift ist selbst der Teufel wohl,
Der uns die lieben Kinder stohl. 40

* * * * *

Das fahrende Fräulein

„O weh der Zeit, die ich verzehrt
Mit meiner Buhler Orden!
Nachreu ist worden mein Gefährt,
Ich bin zur Törin worden.

Mich reut die Schmink und falscher Fleiß, 5
Den ich darauf gewendet,
Die Sonne schien, ich baut' auf Eis,
So war ich schier verblendet.

Wie wird es heiß, fort zieht das Eis
Und meine goldnen Schlösser, 10
Wie ruft es doch im Flusse leis,
Da drunten wär es besser."

Und wie sie in das Wasser fällt,
Da hat sie festgehalten
Der Liebste, dem sie nachgestellt, 15
An ihres Schleiers Falten.

[52]

„Laß mir den Schleier, halt mich nicht,
Laß still mich 'nunter ziehen,
Denn mein verstörtes Angesicht,
Das würde nach dich ziehen."   20

Der Strom ist stark, sein Arm zu schwach,
Sie will den Schleier nicht lassen,
So zieht verlorne Liebe nach,
Er wollte sie nicht verlassen.

* * * * *

Doktor Faust

Hört, ihr Christen, mit Verlangen
Nun was Neues ohne Graus,
Wie die eitle Welt tut prangen
Mit Johann dem Doktor Faust;
Von Anhalt war er geboren,   5
Er studiert mit allem Fleiß,
In der Hoffart auferzogen,
Richtet sich nach aller Weis.
Vierzigtausend Geister
Tut er sich zitieren   10
Mit Gewalt aus der Höllen.
Unter diesen war nicht einer,
Der ihm könnt recht tauglich sein
Als der Mephistophiles geschwind,
Wie der Wind   15
Gab er seinen Willen drein.
Geld viel Tausend muß er schaffen,
Viel Pasteten und Konfekt,
Gold und Silber, was er wollt',
Und zu Straßburg schoß er dann   20
Sehr vortrefflich nach der Scheiben,
Daß er haben konnt sein' Freud,
Er tät nach dem Teufel schieben,
Daß er vielmal laut aufschreit.

[53]

Wann er auf der Post tät reiten, 25
Hat er Geister recht geschoren,
Hinten, vorn, auf beiden Seiten,
Den Weg zu pflastern auserkoren;
Kegelschieben auf der Donau
War zu Regensburg sein Freud. 30
Fische fangen nach Verlangen,
Ware sein Ergötzlichkeit.
Wie er auf den heiligen Karfreitag
Zu Jerusalem kam auf die Straß
Wo Christus an dem Kreuzesstamm 35
Hänget ohne Unterlaß,
Dieses zeigt ihm an der Geist,
Daß er wär für uns gestorben
Und das Heil uns hat erworben,
Und man ihm kein' Dank erweist. 40
Mephistophles geschwind wie der Wind
Mußte gleich so eilend fort
Und ihm bringen drei Elle Leinwand
Von einem gewissen Ort.
Kaum da solches ausgeredt, 45
Waren sie schon wirklich da,
Welche so eilends brachte
Der geschwinde Mephistophila.
Die große Stadt Portugal
Gleich soll abgemalet sein; 50
Dieses geschah auch geschwind
Wie der Wind:
Dann er malt überall
So gleichförmig
Wie die schönste Stadt Portugal. 55
„Hör, du sollst mir jetzt abmalen
Christus an dem heiligen Kreuz;
Was an ihm nur ist zu malen,
Darf nicht fehlen, ich sag es frei,
Daß du nicht fehlst an dem Titul 60
Und dem heiligen Namen sein."
Diesen konnt er nicht abmalen,
Darum bitt' er Faustum
Ganz inständig: „Schlag mir ab

[54]

Nicht mein' Bitt', ich will dir wiederum 65
Geben dein zuvor gegebene Handschrift.
Dann es ist mir unmöglich,
Daß ich schreib: Herr Jesu Christ."
Der Teufel fing an zu fragen:
„Herr, was gibst du für einen Lohn? 70
Hättst das lieber bleiben lassen,
Bei Gott findst du kein Pardon."
Doktor Faust, tu dich bekehren,
Weil du Zeit hast noch ein Stund,
Gott will dir ja jetzt mitteilen 75
Die ew'ge wahre Huld;
Doktor Faust, tu dich bekehren,
Halt du nur ja dieses aus.
„Nach Gott tu ich nichts fragen
Und nach seinem himmlischen Haus!" 80
In derselben Viertelstunde
Kam ein Engel von Gott gesandt,
Der tät so fröhlich singen
Mit einem englischen Lobgesang.
Solang der Engel da gewesen, 85
Wollt sich bekehren Doktor Faust.
Er täte sich alsbald umkehren,
Sehet an den Höllengraus;
Der Teufel hatte ihn verblendet,
Malt ihm ab ein Venusbild, 90
Die bösen Geister verschwunden
Und führten ihn mit in die Höll.

* * * * *

Wenn ich ein Vöglein wär

Wenn ich ein Vöglein wär,
Und auch zwei Flüglein hätt,
Flög ich zu dir;
Weils aber nicht kann sein,
Bleib ich allhier.   5

Bin ich gleich weit von dir,
Bin ich doch im Schlaf bei dir,
Und red mit dir;
Wenn ich erwachen tu,
Bin ich allein.   10

Es vergeht keine Stund in der Nacht,
Da mein Herze nicht erwacht,
Und an dich gedenkt,
Daß du mir viel tausendmal
Dein Herze geschenkt.   15

* * * * *

Wär ich ein Knab geboren

Es wollt ein Mädel grasen,
Wollt grasen im grünen Klee,
Begegnet's ihm ein Reiter,
Wollt's haben zu der Eh.

"Ach komm, du hurtig Mädel,   5
Und setz dich zu mir her."
"Ach wollt, ich dürft mich setzen,
Kein Gras hats Zicklein mehr."

Der Reiter spreit' den Mantel
Wohl über den grünen Klee: 10
"Komm, du mein wackeres Mädel,
Und setz dich zu mir her."

[56]

"Ich wollt, ich dürfte sitzen,
Das Zicklein hat kein Gras,
Hab gar ein zornig Mutter,   15
Sie schlägt mich alle Tag."

"Hast du ein zornig Mutter,
Und schlägt dich alle Tag,
Verbind den kleinen Finger
Und sag, er sei dir ab."   20

"Wie wollt ich dürfen lügen,
Steht mir gar übel an,
Viel lieber wollt ich sprechen,
Der Ritter wär mein Mann." —

"Ach Mutter, liebe Mutter,   25
Ach gebt mir einen Rat,
Es reitet mir alle Tage
Ein hurtiger Ritter nach."

"Ach Tochter! liebe Tochter!
Den Rat, den geb ich dir,   30
Laß du den Reiter fahren,
Bleib du das Jahr bei mir."

"Ach Mutter! liebe Mutter!
Der Rat, der ist nicht gut,
Der Ritter ist mir lieber   35
Als all dein Hab und Gut."

"Ist dir der Reiter lieber
Als all mein Hab und Gut,
So bind dein' Kleid' zusammen
Und lauf dem Reiter zu."   40

"Ach Mutter! liebe Mutter!
Der Kleider hab ich nicht viel,
Gib mir nur hundert Taler,
So kauf ich, was ich will."

"Ach Tochter! liebe Tochter!   45
Der Taler hab ich nicht viel,
Dein Vater hat's verruschelt
In Würfel- und Kartenspiel."

"Hat's denn mein Vater verruschelt
In Würfel- und Kartenspiel,   50
So sei es Gott erbarmet,
Daß ich sein Tochter bin.

Wär ich ein Knab geboren,
Ich wollte ziehn ins Feld,
Ich wollt die Trommel rühren   55
Dem Kaiser um sein Geld."

* * * * *

Laß rauschen, Lieb, laß rauschen!

Ich hört ein Sichlein rauschen,
Wohl rauschen durch das Korn,
Ich hört ein Mägdlein klagen,
Sie hätt ihr Lieb verlorn.

Laß rauschen, Lieb, laß rauschen,   5
Ich acht nicht, wie es geht,
Ich tät mein Lieb vertauschen
In Veilchen und im Klee.

Du hast ein Mägdlein worben
In Veilchen und im Klee,   10
So steh ich hier alleine,
Tut meinem Herzen weh.

Ich hör ein Hirschlein rauschen,
Wohl rauschen durch den Wald,
Ich hör mein Lieb sich klagen,   15
Die Lieb verrauscht so bald.

[58]

Laß rauschen, Lieb, laß rauschen,
Ich weiß nicht, wie mir wird,
Die Bächlein immer rauschen,
Und keines sich verirrt.   20

* * * * *

Ikarus

Mir träumt, ich flög gar bange
Wohl in die Welt hinaus,
Zu Straßburg durch alle Gassen
Bis vor Feinsliebchens Haus.

Feinsliebchen ist betrübt,   5
Als ich so flieg, und rennt:
„Wer dich so fliegen lehrt,
Das ist der böse Feind."

„Feinsliebchen, was hilft hier lügen,
Da du doch alles weißt,   10
Wer mich so fliegen lehrt,
Das ist der böse Geist." ·

Feinsliebchen weint und schreiet,
Daß ich vom Schrei erwacht,
Da saß ich, ach! in Augsburg   15
Gefangen auf der Wacht.

Und morgen muß ich hangen,
Feinslieb mich nicht mehr ruft,
Wohl morgen als ein Vogel
Schwank ich in freier Luft.   20

[59]

Ludwig Uhland

(1787–1862)

The portrait of Uhland on the previous page is based on a painting by Christian Friedrich Dörr (1810).

Bauernregel

Im Sommer such ein Liebchen dir
In Garten und Gefild!
Da sind die Tage lang genug,
Da sind die Nächte mild.

Im Winter muß der süße Bund   5
Schon fest geschlossen sein,
So darfst nicht lange stehn im Schnee
Bei kaltem Mondenschein.

* * * * *

Hans und Grete

SIE
Guckst du mir denn immer nach,
Wo du nur mich findest?
Nimm die Äuglein doch in acht!
Daß du nicht erblindest.

ER
Gucktest du nicht stets herum,   5
Würdest mich nicht sehen;
Nimm dein Hälschen doch in acht!
Wirst es noch verdrehen.

* * * * *

Der Wirtin Töchterlein

Es zogen drei Bursche wohl über den Rhein,
Bei einer Frau Wirtin, da kehrten sie ein.

[63]

"Frau Wirtin! hat Sie gut Bier und Wein?
Wo hat Sie Ihr schönes Töchterlein?"

"Mein Bier und Wein ist frisch und klar,   5
Mein Töchterlein liegt auf der Totenbahr."

Und als sie traten zur Kammer hinein,
Da lag sie in einem schwarzen Schrein.

Der erste, der schlug den Schleier zurück
Und schaute sie an mit traurigem Blick: 10

"Ach! lebtest du noch, du schöne Maid!
Ich würde dich lieben von dieser Zeit."

Der zweite deckte den Schleier zu
Und kehrte sich ab und weinte dazu:

"Ach! daß du liegst auf der Totenbahr!   15
Ich hab dich geliebet so manches Jahr."

Der dritte hub ihn wieder sogleich
Und küßte sie an den Mund so bleich:

"Dich lieb' ich immer, dich lieb ich noch heut
Und werde dich lieben in Ewigkeit."   20

* * * * *

Frühlingsglaube

Die linden Lüfte sind erwacht,
Sie säuseln und weben Tag und Nacht,
Sie schaffen an allen Enden.
O frischer Duft, o neuer Klang!
Nun, armes Herze, sei nicht bang!   5
Nun muß sich alles, alles wenden.

[64]

Die Welt wird schöner mit jedem Tag,
Man weiß nicht, was noch werden mag,
Das Blühen will nicht enden.
Es blüht das fernste, tiefste Tal: 10
Nun, armes Herz, vergiß der Qual!
Nun muß sich alles, alles wenden.

* * * * *

Frühlingslied des Rezensenten

Frühling ist's, ich laß es gelten,
Und mich freut's, ich muß gestehen,
Daß man kann spazieren gehen,
Ohne just sich zu erkälten.

Störche kommen an und Schwalben,   5
Nicht zu frühe, nicht zu frühe!
Blühe nur, mein Bäumchen, blühe!
Meinethalben, meinethalben!

Ja! ich fühl ein wenig Wonne,
Denn die Lerche singt erträglich,   10
Philomele nicht alltäglich,
Nicht so übel scheint die Sonne.

Daß es keinen überrasche,
Mich im grünen Feld zu sehen!
Nicht verschmäh ich auszugehen,   15
Kleistens Frühling in der Tasche.

* * * * *

[65]

Romanze vom Rezensenten

Rezensent, der tapfre Ritter,
Steigt zu Rosse, kühn und stolz;
Ist's kein Hengst aus Andalusien,
Ist es doch ein Bock von Holz.
Statt des Schwerts die scharfe Feder   5
Zieht er kampfbereit vom Ohr,
Schiebt statt des Visiers die Brille
Den entbrannten Augen vor.
Publikum, die edle Dame,
Schwebt in tausendfacher Not,   10
Seit ihr bald, barbarisch schnaubend,
Ein Siegfriedscher Lindwurm droht,
Bald ein süßer Sonettiste
Sie mit Lautenklimpern lockt,
Bald ein Mönch ihr mystisch predigt,   15
Daß ihr die Besinnung stockt.
Rezensent, der tapfre Ritter,
Hält sich gut im Drachenmord,
Schlägt in Splitter alle Lauten,
Stürzt den Mönch vom Kanzelbord.   20
Dennoch will er, groß bescheiden,
Daß ihn niemand nennen soll,
Und den Schild des Helden zeichnet
Kaum ein Schriftzug rätselvoll.
Rezensent, du Hort der Schwachen,   25
Sei uns immer treu und hold!
Nimm zum Lohn des Himmels Segen,
Des Verlegers Ehrensold!

* * * * *

Der Mohn

Wie dort, gewiegt von Westen,
Des Mohnes Blüte glänzt!
Die Blume, die am besten
Des Traumgotts Schläfe kränzt;
Bald purpurhell, als spiele   5
Der Abendröte Schein,
Bald weiß und bleich, als fiele
Des Mondes Schimmer ein.

Zur Warnung hört ich sagen,
Daß, der im Mohne schlief,   10
Hinunter ward getragen
In Träume, schwer und tief;
Dem Wachen selbst geblieben
Sei irren Wahnes Spur,
Die Nahen und die Lieben   15
Halt' er für Schemen nur.

In meiner Tage Morgen,
Da lag ich auch einmal,
Von Blumen ganz verborgen,
In einem schönen Tal.   20
Sie dufteten so milde!
Da ward, ich fühlt es kaum,
Das Leben mir zum Bilde,
Das Wirkliche zum Traum.

Seitdem ist mir beständig,   25
Als wär es so nur recht,
Mein Bild der Welt lebendig,
Mein Traum nur wahr und echt;
Die Schatten, die ich sehe,
Sie sind wie Sterne klar.   30
O Mohn der Dichtung! wehe
Ums Haupt mir immerdar!

* * * * *

Die Ulme zu Hirsau

Zu Hirsau in den Trümmern,
Da wiegt ein Ulmenbaum
Frischgrünend seine Krone
Hoch überm Giebelsaum.

Er wurzelt tief im Grunde   5
Vom alten Klosterbau,
Er wölbt sich statt des Daches
Hinaus in Himmelsblau.

Weil des Gemäuers Enge
Ihm Luft und Sonne nahm,   10
So trieb's ihn hoch und höher,
Bis er zum Lichte kam.

Es ragen die vier Wände,
Als ob sie nur bestimmt,
Den kühnen Wuchs zu schirmen,   15
Der zu den Wolken klimmt.

Wenn dort im grünen Tale
Ich einsam mich erging,
Die Ulme war's, die hehre,
Woran mein Sinnen hing.   20

Wenn in dem dumpfen, stummen
Getrümmer ich gelauscht,
Da hat ihr reger Wipfel
Im Windesflug gerauscht.

Ich sah ihn oft erglühen   25
Im ersten Morgenstrahl;
Ich sah ihn noch erleuchtet,
Wann schattig rings das Tal.

Zu Wittenberg im Kloster
Wuchs auch ein solcher Strauß   30
Und brach mit Riesenästen
Zum Klausendach hinaus.

O Strahl des Lichts! du dringest
Hinab in jede Gruft.
O Geist der Welt! du ringest   35
Hinauf in Licht und Luft.

* * * * *

Das Glück von Edenhall

Von Edenhall der junge Lord
Läßt schmettern Festtrommetenschall,
Er hebt sich an des Tisches Bord
Und ruft in trunkner Gäste Schwall:
,,Nun her mit dem Glücke von Edenhall!''   5

Der Schenk vernimmt ungern den Spruch,
Des Hauses ältester Vasall,
Nimmt zögernd aus dem seidnen Tuch
Das hohe Trinkglas von Kristall,
Sie nennen's: *das Glück von Edenhall.*   10

Darauf der Lord: ,,Dem Glas zum Preis
Schenk roten ein aus Portugal!''
Mit Händezittern gießt der Greis,
Und purpurn Licht wird überall,
Es strahlt aus dem Glücke von Edenhall.   15

Da spricht der Lord und schwingt's dabei:
,,Dies Glas von leuchtendem Kristall
Gab meinem Ahn am Quell die Fei,
Drein schrieb sie: kommt dies Glas zu Fall,
Fahr wohl dann, o Glück von Edenhall!   20

[69]

Ein Kelchglas war zum Los mit Fug
Dem freud'gen Stamm von Edenhall;
Wir schlürfen gern in vollem Zug,
Wir läuten gern mit lautem Schall;
Stoßt an mit dem Glücke von Edenhall!''   25

Erst klingt es milde, tief und voll,
Gleich dem Gesang der Nachtigall,
Dann wie des Waldstroms laut Geroll,
Zuletzt erdröhnt wie Donnerhall
Das herrliche Glück von Edenhall.   30

''Zum Horte nimmt ein kühn Geschlecht
Sich den zerbrechlichen Kristall;
Er dauert länger schon als recht,
Stoßt an! mit diesem kräft'gen Prall
Versuch ich das Glück von Edenhall.''   35

Und als das Trinkglas gellend springt,
Springt das Gewölb mit jähem Knall,
Und aus dem Riß die Flamme dringt;
Die Gäste sind zerstoben all
Mit dem brechenden Glücke von Edenhall.   40

Ein stürmt der Feind mit Brand und Mord,
Der in der Nacht erstieg den Wall,
Vom Schwerte fällt der junge Lord,
Hält in der Hand noch den Kristall,
Das zersprungene Glück von Edenhall.   45

Am Morgen irrt der Schenk allein,
Der Greis, in der zerstörten Hall,
Er sucht des Herrn verbrannt Gebein,
Er sucht im grausen Trümmerfall
Die Scherben des Glücks von Edenhall.   50

''Die Steinwand'', spricht er, ''springt zu Stück,
Die hohe Säule muß zu Fall,
Glas ist der Erde Stolz und Glück,
In Splitter fällt der Erdenball
Einst gleich dem Glücke von Edenhall.''   55

Joseph von Eichendorff
(1788–1857)

The portrait of Eichendorff on the previous page is based on a drawing by Franz Kugler (1832).

Abschied

O Täler weit, o Höhen,
O schöner, grüner Wald,
Du meiner Lust und Wehen
Andächt'ger Aufenthalt!
Da draußen, stets betrogen,   5
Saust die geschäft'ge Welt,
Schlag noch einmal die Bogen
Um mich, du grünes Zelt!

Wenn es beginnt zu tagen,
Die Erde dampft und blinkt,   10
Die Vögel lustig schlagen,
Daß dir dein Herz erklingt:
Da mag vergehn, verwehen
Das trübe Erdenleid,
Da sollst du auferstehen   15
In junger Herrlichkeit!

Da steht im Wald geschrieben
Ein stilles, ernstes Wort
Von rechtem Tun und Lieben,
Und was des Menschen Hort.   20
Ich habe treu gelesen
Die Worte schlicht und wahr,
Und durch mein ganzes Wesen
Ward's unaussprechlich klar.

Bald werd ich dich verlassen,   25
Fremd in der Fremde gehn,
Auf buntbewegten Gassen
Des Lebens Schauspiel sehn;
Und mitten in dem Leben
Wird deines Ernsts Gewalt   30
Mich Einsamen erheben,
So wird mein Herz nicht alt.

* * * * *

[73]

Das zerbrochene Ringlein

In einem kühlen Grunde
Da geht ein Mühlenrad,
Mein' Liebste ist verschwunden,
Die dort gewohnet hat.

Sie hat mir Treu versprochen,   5
Gab mir ein'n Ring dabei,
Sie hat die Treu gebrochen,
Mein Ringlein sprang entzwei.

Ich möcht als Spielmann reisen
Weit in die Welt hinaus,   10
Und singen meine Weisen,
Und gehn von Haus zu Haus.

Ich möcht als Reiter fliegen
Wohl in die blut'ge Schlacht,
Um stille Feuer liegen ·   15
Im Feld bei dunkler Nacht.

Hör ich das Mühlrad gehen:
Ich weiß nicht, was ich will —
Ich möcht am liebsten sterben,
Da wär's auf einmal still!   20

* * * * *

Zwielicht

Dämmrung will die Flügel spreiten,
Schaurig rühren sich die Bäume,
Wolken ziehn wie schwere Träume —
Was will dieses Graun bedeuten?

[74]

Hast ein Reh du lieb vor andern, 5
Laß es nicht alleine grasen,
Jäger ziehn im Wald und blasen,
Stimmen hin und wieder wandern.

Hast du einen Freund hienieden,
Trau ihm nicht zu dieser Stunde, 10
Freundlich wohl mit Aug und Munde,
Sinnt er Krieg im tück'schen Frieden.

Was heut müde gehet unter,
Hebt sich morgen neugeboren.
Manches bleibt in Nacht verloren — 15
Hüte dich, bleib wach und munter!

* * * * *

Der frohe Wandersmann

Wem Gott will rechte Gunst erweisen,
Den schickt er in die weite Welt;
Dem will er seine Wunder weisen
In Berg und Wald und Strom und Feld.

Die Trägen, die zu Hause liegen, 5
Erquicket nicht das Morgenrot,
Sie wissen nur von Kinderwiegen,
Von Sorgen, Last und Not um Brot.

Die Bächlein von den Bergen springen,
Die Lerchen schwirren hoch vor Lust, 10
Was sollt ich nicht mit ihnen singen
Aus voller Kehl' und frischer Brust?

Den lieben Gott laß ich nur walten;
Der Bächlein, Lerchen, Wald und Feld
Und Erd' und Himmel will erhalten, 15
Hat auch mein' Sach' aufs best' bestellt!

[75]

* * * * *

Sehnsucht

Es schienen so golden die Sterne,
Am Fenster ich einsam stand
Und hörte aus weiter Ferne
Ein Posthorn im stillen Land.
Das Herz mir im Leib entbrennte,   5
Da hab ich mir heimlich gedacht:
Ach, wer da mitreisen könnte
In der prächtigen Sommernacht!

Zwei junge Gesellen gingen
Vorüber am Bergeshang,   10
Ich hörte im Wandern sie singen
Die stille Gegend entlang:
Von schwindelnden Felsenschlüften,
Wo die Wälder rauschen so sacht,
Von Quellen, die von den Klüften   15
Sich stürzen in die Waldesnacht.

Sie sangen von Marmorbildern,
Von Gärten, die überm Gestein
In dämmernden Lauben verwildern,
Palästen im Mondenschein,   20
Wo die Mädchen am Fenster lauschen,
Wann der Lauten Klang erwacht
Und die Brunnen verschlafen rauschen
In der prächtigen Sommernacht. —

* * * * *

Wünschelrute

Schläft ein Lied in allen Dingen,
Die da träumen fort und fort,
Und die Welt hebt an zu singen,
Triffst du nur das Zauberwort.

* * * * *

Zauberblick

Die Burg, die liegt verfallen
In schöner Einsamkeit,
Dort saß ich vor den Hallen
Bei stiller Mittagszeit.

Es ruhten in der Kühle   5
Die Rehe auf dem Wall
Und tief in blauer Schwüle
Die sonn'gen Täler all.

Tief unten hört ich Glocken
In weiter Ferne gehn,   10
Ich aber mußt' erschrocken
Zum alten Erker sehn.

Denn in dem Fensterbogen
Ein' schöne Fraue stand,
Als hütete sie droben   15
Die Wälder und das Land.

Ihr Haar, wie'n goldner Mantel,
War tief herabgerollt;
Auf einmal sie sich wandte,
Als ob sie sprechen wollt.   20

[77]

Und als ich schauernd lauschte —
Da war ich aufgewacht,
Und unter mir schon rauschte
So wunderbar die Nacht.

Träumt ich im Mondesschimmer?   25
Ich weiß nicht, was mir graut,
Doch das vergeß ich nimmer,
Wie sie mich angeschaut!

Heinrich Heine
(1797–1856)

The portrait of Heine on the previous page is based on a drawing by Ludwig Grimm (1827).

Belsatzar

Die Mitternacht zog näher schon;
In stummer Ruh lag Babylon.

Nur oben in des Königs Schloß,
Da flackerts, da lärmt des Königs Troß.

Dort oben in dem Königssaal   5
Belsatzar hielt sein Königsmahl.

Die Knechte saßen in schimmernden Reihn
Und leerten die Becher mit funkelndem Wein.

Es klirrten die Becher, es jauchzten die Knecht';
So klang es dem störrigen Könige recht.   10

Des Königs Wangen leuchten Glut;
Im Wein erwuchs ihm kecker Mut.

Und blindlings reißt der Mut ihn fort;
Und er lästert die Gottheit mit sündigem Wort.

Und er brüstet sich frech, und lästert wild;   15
Die Knechtenschar ihm Beifall brüllt.

Der König rief mit stolzem Blick;
Der Diener eilt und kehrt zurück.

Er trug viel gülden Gerät auf dem Haupt;
Das war aus dem Tempel Jehovahs geraubt.   20

Und der König ergriff mit frevler Hand
Einen heiligen Becher, gefüllt bis am Rand.

Und er leert ihn hastig bis auf den Grund,
Und rufet laut mit schäumendem Mund:

Jehovah! dir künd' ich auf ewig Hohn —   25
Ich bin der König von Babylon!

[81]

Doch kaum das grause Wort verklang,
Dem König wards heimlich im Busen bang.

Das gellende Lachen verstummte zumal;
Es wurde leichenstill im Saal.   30

Und sieh! und sieh! an weißer Wand
Da kams hervor wie Menschenhand;

Und schrieb, und schrieb an weißer Wand
Buchstaben von Feuer, und schrieb und schwand.

Der König stieren Blicks da saß,   35
Mit schlotternden Knien und totenblaß.

Die Knechtenschar saß kalt durchgraut,
Und saß gar still, gab keinen Laut.

Die Magier kamen, doch keiner verstand
Zu deuten die Flammenschrift an dèr Wand.   40

Belsatzar ward aber in selbiger Nacht
Von seinen Knechten umgebracht.

* * * * *

Im wunderschönen Monat Mai,
Als alle Knospen sprangen,
Da ist in meinem Herzen
Die Liebe aufgegangen.

Im wunderschönen Monat Mai,   5
Als alle Vögel sangen,
Da hab ich ihr gestanden
Mein Sehnen und Verlangen.

* * * * *

[82]

Ein Fichtenbaum steht einsam
Im Norden auf kahler Höh.
Ihn schläfert; mit weißer Decke
Umhüllen ihn Eis und Schnee.

Er träumt von einer Palme,   5
Die, fern im Morgenland,
Einsam und schweigend trauert
Auf brennender Felsenwand.

* * * * *

Ein Jüngling liebt ein Mädchen,
Die hat einen andern erwählt;
Der andre liebt eine andre,
Und hat sich mit dieser vermählt.

Das Mädchen heiratet aus Ärger   5
Den ersten besten Mann,
Der ihr in den Weg gelaufen;
Der Jüngling ist übel dran.

Es ist eine alte Geschichte,
Doch bleibt sie immer neu;   10
Und wem sie just passieret,
Dem bricht das Herz entzwei.

* * * * *

Aus alten Märchen winkt es
Hervor mit weißer Hand,
Da singt es und da klingt es
Von einem Zauberland:

Wo große Blumen schmachten   5
Im goldnen Abendlicht,
Und zärtlich sich betrachten
Mit bräutlichem Gesicht; —

Wo alle Bäume sprechen
Und singen, wie ein Chor,   10
Und laute Quellen brechen
Wie Tanzmusik hervor; —

Und Liebesweisen tönen,
Wie du sie nie gehört,
Bis wundersüßes Sehnen   15
Dich wundersüß betört!

Ach, könnt ich dorthin kommen,
Und dort mein Herz erfreun,
Und aller Qual entnommen,
Und frei und selig sein!   20

Ach! jenes Land der Wonne,
Das seh ich oft im Traum;
Doch kommt die Morgensonne,
Zerfließts wie eitel Schaum.

* * * * *

Sie saßen und tranken am Teetisch,
Und sprachen von Liebe viel.
Die Herren die waren ästhetisch,
Die Damen von zartem Gefühl.

Die Liebe muß sein platonisch,   5
Der dürre Hofrat sprach.
Die Hofrätin lächelt ironisch,
Und dennoch seufzet sie: Ach!

Der Domherr öffnet den Mund weit:
Die Liebe sei nicht zu roh,   10
Sie schadet sonst der Gesundheit.
Das Fräulein lispelt: Wie so?

Die Gräfin spricht wehmütig:
Die Liebe ist eine Passion!
Und präsentieret gütig   15
Die Tasse dem Herrn Baron.

Am Tische war noch ein Plätzchen;
Mein Liebchen, da hast du gefehlt.
Du hättest so hübsch, mein Schätzchen,
Von deiner Liebe erzählt.   20

* * * * *

Ich weiß nicht, was soll es bedeuten,
Daß ich so traurig bin;
Ein Märchen aus alten Zeiten,
Das kommt mir nicht aus dem Sinn.

Die Luft ist kühl und es dunkelt,   5
Und ruhig fließt der Rhein;
Der Gipfel des Berges funkelt
Im Abendsonnenschein.

Die schönste Jungfrau sitzet
Dort oben wunderbar,   10
Ihr gold'nes Geschmeide blitzet,
Sie kämmt ihr goldenes Haar.

Sie kämmt es mit goldenem Kamme
Und singt ein Lied dabei;
Das hat eine wundersame,   15
Gewaltige Melodei.

Den Schiffer im kleinen Schiffe
Ergreift es mit wildem Weh;
Er schaut nicht die Felsenriffe,
Er schaut nur hinauf in die Höh.   20

Ich glaube, die Wellen verschlingen
Am Ende Schiffer und Kahn;
Und das hat mit ihrem Singen
Die Lore-Ley getan.

* * * * *

Meeresstille

Meeresstille! Ihre Strahlen
Wirft die Sonne auf das Wasser,
Und im wogenden Geschmeide
Zieht das Schiff die grünen Furchen.

Bei dem Steuer liegt der Bootsmann   5
Auf dem Bauch und schnarchet leise.
Bei dem Mastbaum, segelflickend,
Kauert der beteerte Schifsjung.

Hinter'm Schmutze seiner Wangen
Sprüht es rot, wehmütig zuckt es   10
Um das breite Maul, und schmerzlich
Schaun die großen, schönen Augen.

[86]

Denn der Kapitän steht vor ihm,
Tobt und flucht und schilt ihn: Spitzbub.
„Spitzbub! einen Hering hast du   15
Aus der Tonne mir gestohlen!"

Meeresstille! Aus den Wellen
Taucht hervor ein kluges Fischlein,
Wärmt das Köpfchen in der Sonne,
Plätschert lustig mit dem Schwänzchen.   20

Doch die Möwe, aus den Lüften,
Schießt herunter auf das Fischlein,
Und, den raschen Raub im Schnabel,
Schwingt sie sich hinauf ins Blaue.

*   *   *   *   *

Das Fräulein stand am Meere
Und seufzte lang und bang,
Es rührte sie so sehre
Der Sonnenuntergang.

Mein Fräulein! sein sie munter,   5
Das ist ein altes Stück,
Hier vorne geht sie unter
Und kehrt von hinten zurück.

*   *   *   *   *

Im Mai

Die Freunde, die ich geküßt und geliebt,
Die haben das Schlimmste an mir verübt.
Mein Herze bricht; doch droben die Sonne,
Lachend begrüßt sie den Monat der Wonne.

Es blüht der Lenz. Im grünen Wald   5
Der lustige Vogelgesang erschallt,
Und Mädchen und Blumen, sie lächeln jungfräulich —
O schöne Welt, du bist abscheulich!

Da lob ich mir den Orkus fast;
Dort kränkt uns nirgends ein schnöder Kontrast;   10
Für leidende Herzen ist es viel besser
Dort unten am stygischen Nachtgewässer.

Sein melancholisches Geräusch,
Der Stymphaliden ödes Gekreisch,
Der Furien Singsang, so schrill und grell,   15
Dazwischen des Cerberus Gebell —

Das paßt verdrießlich zu Unglück und Qual —
Im Schattenreich, dem traurigen Tal,
In Proserpinens verdammten Domänen,
Ist alles im Einklang mit unseren Tränen.   20

Hier oben aber — wie grausamlich
Sonne und Rosen stechen sie mich!
Mich höhnt der Himmel, der bläulich und mailich —
O schöne Welt, du bist abscheulich!

[88]

Nikolaus Lenau
(1802–50)

Nicolaus Lenau.

The portrait of Lenau on the previous page is based on an anonymous engraving.

Bitte

Weil auf mir, du dunkles Auge,
Übe deine ganze Macht,
Ernste, milde, träumerische,
Unergründlich süße Nacht!

Nimm mit denem Zauberdunkel   5
Diese Welt von hinnen mir,
Daß du über meinem Leben
Einsam schwebest für und für.

* * * * *

Der Postillion

Lieblich war die Maiennacht,
Silberwölklein flogen,
Ob der holden Frühlingspracht
Freudig hingezogen.

Schlummernd lagen Wies und Hain,   5
Jeder Pfad verlassen;
Niemand als der Mondenschein
Wachte auf der Straßen.

Leise nur das Lüftchen sprach,
Und es zog gelinder   10
Durch das stille Schlafgemach
All der Frühlingskinder.

Heimlich nur das Bächlein schlich,
Denn der Blüten Träume
Dufteten gar wonniglich   15
Durch die stillen Räume.

Rauher war mein Postillion,
Ließ die Geißel knallen,
Über Berg und Tal davon
Frisch sein Horn erschallen.   20

Und von flinken Rossen vier
Scholl der Hufe Schlagen,
Die durchs blühende Revier
Trabten mit Behagen.

Wald und Flur im schnellen Zug   25
Kaum gegrüßt — gemieden;
Und vorbei, wie Traumesflug,
Schwand der Dörfer Frieden.

Mitten in dem Maienglück
Lag ein Kirchhof innen,   30
Der den raschen Wanderblick
Hielt zu ernstem Sinnen.

Hingelehnt an Bergesrand
War die bleiche Mauer,
Und das Kreuzbild Gottes stand   35
Hoch, in stummer Trauer.

Schwager ritt auf seiner Bahn
Stiller jetzt und trüber;
Und die Rosse hielt er an,
Sah zum Kreuz hinüber: 40

„Halten muß hier Roß und Rad,
Mags euch nicht gefährden:
Drüben liegt mein Kamerad
In der kühlen Erden!

Ein gar herzlieber Gesell!   45
Herr, 's ist ewig schade!
Keiner blies das Horn so hell
Wie mein Kamerade!

[92]

Hier ich immer halten muß,
Dem dort unterm Rasen   50
Zum getreuen Brudergruß
Sein Leiblied zu blasen!"

Und dem Kirchhof sandt er zu
Frohe Wandersänge,
Daß es in die Grabesruh   55
Seinem Bruder dränge.

Und des Hornes heller Ton
Klang vom Berge wieder,
Ob der tote Postillion
Stimmt' in seine Lieder. —   60

Weiter gings durch Feld und Hag
Mit verhängtem Zügel;
Lang mir noch im Ohre lag
Jener Klang vom Hügel.

* * * * *

Die drei Indianer

Mächtig zürnt der Himmel im Gewitter,
Schmettert manche Rieseneich in Splitter,
Übertönt des Niagara Stimme,
Und mit seiner Blitze Flammenruten
Peitscht er schneller die beschäumten Fluten,   5
Daß sie stürzen mit empörtem Grimme.

Indianer stehn am lauten Strande,
Lauschen nach dem wilden Wogenbrande,
Nach des Waldes bangem Sterbgestöhne;
Greis der eine, mit ergrautem Haare,   10
Aufrecht überragend seine Jahre,
Die zwei andern seïne starken Söhne.

[93]

Seine Söhne jetzt der Greis betrachtet,
Und sein Blick sich dunkler jetzt umnachtet
Als die Wolken, die den Himmel schwärzen,   15
Und sein Aug versendet wildre Blitze
Als das Wetter durch die Wolkenritze,
Und er spricht aus tiefempörtem Herzen:

„Fluch den Weißen! ihren letzten Spuren!
Jeder Welle Fluch, worauf sie fuhren,   20
Die einst Bettler unsern Strand erklettert!
Fluch dem Windhauch, dienstbar ihrem Schiffe!
Hundert Flüche jedem Felsenriffe,
Das sie nicht hat in den Grund geschmettert!

Täglich übers Meer in wilder Eile   25
Fliegen ihre Schiffe, giftge Pfeile,
Treffen unsre Küste mit Verderben.
Nichts hat uns die Räuberbrut gelassen,
Als im Herzen tödlich bittres Hassen:
Kommt, ihr Kinder, kommt, wir wollen sterben!"   30

Also sprach der Alte, und sie schneiden
Ihren Nachen von den Uferweiden,
Drauf sie nach des Stromes Mitte ringen;
Und nun werfen sie weithin die Ruder,
Armverschlungen Vater, Sohn und Bruder   35
Stimmen an, ihr Sterbelied zu singen.

Laut ununterbrochne Donner krachen,
Blitze flattern um den Todesnachen,
Ihn umtaumeln Möwen sturmesmunter;
Und die Männer kommen festentschlossen   40
Singend schon dem Falle zugeschossen,
Stürzen jetzt den Katarakt hinunter.

* * * * *

Stimme des Windes

In Schlummer ist der dunkle Wald gesunken,
Zu träge ist die Luft, ein Blatt zu neigen,
Den Blütenduft zu tragen, und es schweigen
Im Laub die Vögel und im Teich die Unken.

Leuchtkäfer nur, wie stille Traumesfunken   5
Den Schlaf durchgaukelnd, schimmern in den Zweigen,
Und süßer Träume ungestörtem Reigen
Ergibt sich meine Seele, schweigenstrunken.

Horch! überraschend saust es in den Bäumen
Und ruft mich ab von meinen lieben Träumen,   10
Ich höre plötzlich ernste Stimme sprechen;

Die aufgeschreckte Seele lauscht dem Winde
Wie Worten ihres Vaters, der dem Kinde
Zuruft, vom Spiele heimwärts aufzubrechen.

Stimme des Regens

Die Lüfte rasten auf der weiten Heide,
Die Disteln sind so regungslos zu schauen,
So starr, als wären sie aus Stein gehauen,
Bis sie der Wandrer streift mit seinem Kleide.

Und Erd und Himmel haben keine Scheide,   5
In eins gefallen sind die nebelgrauen,
Zwei Freunden gleich, die sich ihr Leid vertrauen,
Und Mein und Dein vergessen traurig beide.

Nun plötzlich wankt die Distel hin und wieder,
Und heftig rauschend bricht der Regen nieder,   10
Wie laute Antwort auf ein stummes Fragen.

Der Wandrer hört den Regen niederbrausen,
Er hört die windgepeitschte Distel sausen,
Und eine Wehmut fühlt er, nicht zu sagen.

[95]

Stimme der Glocken

Den glatten See kein Windeshauch verknittert,
Das Hochgebirg, die Tannen, Klippen, Buchten,
Die Gletscher, die von Wolken nur besuchten,
Sie spiegeln sich im Wasser unzersplittert.

Das dürre Blatt vom Baume hörbar zittert,   5
Und hörbar rieselt nieder in die Schluchten
Das kleinste Steinchen, das auf ihren Fluchten
Die Gemse schnellt, wenn sie den Jäger wittert.

Horch! Glocken in der weiten Ferne tönend,
Den Gram mir weckend und zugleich versöhnend,   10
Dort auf der Wiese weiden Alpenkühe.

Das Läuten mahnt mich leise an den Frieden,
Der von der Erd auf immer ist geschieden
Schon in der ersten Paradiesesfrühe.

Stimme des Kindes

Ein schlafend Kind! o still! in diesen Zügen
Könnt ihr das Paradies zurückbeschwören;
Es lächelt süß, als lauscht es Engelchören,
Den Mund umsäuselt himmlisches Vergnügen.

O schweige, Welt, mit deinen lauten Lügen,   5
Die Wahrheit dieses Traumes nicht zu stören!
Laß mich das Kind im Traume sprechen hören
Und mich, vergessend, in die Unschuld fügen!

Das Kind, nicht ahnend mein bewegtes Lauschen,
Mit dunklen Lauten hat mein Herz gesegnet,   10
Mehr als im stillen Wald des Baumes Rauschen;

Ein tiefres Heimweh hat mich überfallen,
Als wenn es auf die stille Heide regnet,
Wenn im Gebirg die fernen Glocken hallen.

[96]

* * * * *

Die drei Zigeuner

Drei Zigeuner fand ich einmal
Liegen an einer Weide,
Als mein Fuhrwerk mit müder Qual
Schlich durch sandige Heide.

Hielt der eine für sich allein   5
In den Händen die Fiedel,
Spielte, umglüht vom Abendschein,
Sich ein feuriges Liedel.

Hielt der zweite die Pfeif im Mund,
Blickte nach seinem Rauche,   10
Froh, als ob er vom Erdenrund
Nichts zum Glücke mehr brauche.

Und der dritte behaglich schlief,
Und sein Zimbal am Baum hing,
Über die Saiten der Windhauch lief,   15
Über sein Herz ein Traum ging.

An den Kleidern trugen die drei
Löcher und bunte Flicken,
Aber sie boten trotzig frei
Spott den Erdengeschicken.   20

Dreifach haben sie mir gezeigt,
Wenn das Leben uns nachtet,
Wie mans verraucht, verschläft, vergeigt
Und es dreimal verachtet.

Nach den Ziegeunern lang noch schaun   25
Mußt ich im Weiterfahren,
Nach den Gesichtern dunkelbraun,
Den schwarzlockigen Haaren.

* * * * *

Herbstgefühl

Der Buchenwald ist herbstlich schon gerötet,
So wie ein Kranker, der sich neigt zum Sterben,
Wenn flüchtig noch sich seine Wangen färben,
Doch Rosen sinds, wobei kein Lied mehr flötet.

Das Bächlein zieht und rieselt, kaum zu hören,   5
Das Tal hinab, und seine Wellen gleiten,
Wie durch das Sterbgemach die Freunde schreiten,
Den letzten Traum des Lebens nicht zu stören.

Ein trüber Wandrer findet hier Genossen,
Es ist Natur, der auch die Freuden schwanden,   10
Mit seiner ganzen Schwermut einverstanden,
Er ist in ihre Klagen eingeschlossen.

Notes

Novalis

Editions

Novalis. Schriften. Edited by Paul Kluckhohn and Richard Samuel, 2nd ed., 4 vols., Darmstadt, 1960–75.

Novalis. Werke. Edited by Gerhard Schulz, 2nd ed., Munich, 1981.

Novalis. Werke in einem Band. Edited by Hans-Joachim Mähl and Richard Samuel, Munich, 1981.

General Reading

Bruce Haywood, *Novalis. The Veil of Imagery*, The Hague, 1959.

Heinz Ritter, *Der unbekannte Novalis. Friedrich von Hardenberg im Spiegel seiner Dichtung*, Göttingen, 1967.

Gerhard Schulz, *Novalis*, Reinbek, 1969 (rowohlts monographien 154).

— (ed.), *Novalis. Beiträge zu Werk und Persönlichkeit Friedrich von Hardenbergs*, Darmstadt, 1970.

Hans-Joachim Mähl, 'Friedrich von Hardenberg (Novalis)', in Benno von Wiese (ed.), *Deutsche Dichter der Romantik*, 2nd ed., Berlin, 1983, pp. 224–59.

Josef Haslinger, *Die Ästhetik des Novalis*, Hain, 1981.

Life

Of all the German poets of the Romantic epoch, Novalis is the one who comes closest to epitomising the values and aspirations of the movement. His impassioned and often fragmentary writings are dominated by an unswerving pursuit of an other-worldly harmony, as his life was by a longing for an early death, which he believed would not only return him to the fountain-head of life, but also unite him with the child bride he had lost through a tragic illness. He was a scholar and a scientist as well as a poet and novelist. His works include essays, aphorisms, hymns, and prose meditations. For a long time it was customary to see him as a mystic and a dreamer, a 'divine youth' whose meteoric career reflected the self-destructive intensity of true genius. More recently, he has been hailed as the precursor of literary modernism; Hofmannsthal, Musil, Broch and many other twentieth-century writers have paid tribute to his influence.

Born Georg Friedrich Philipp von Hardenberg, but now universally known by his apt pseudonym Novalis ('cultivator of new ground'), he spent his youth in Saxony and became acquainted with Schiller and

Friedrich Schlegel while at the universities of Jena and Leipzig. In November 1794, having completed his studies and taken up an administrative post in Bad Tennstedt, he fell in love with Sophie von Kühn, an attractive, quick-witted and evidently precocious girl who, at the time of their betrothal in the following spring, had just turned thirteen years of age. Through his reading of Fichte and the Pietists as much as through contact with Sophie, Novalis became fascinated by the idea of an all-penetrating, universal love ('die unendliche Idee der Liebe'), which was at once secular and religious, physical and spiritual, and to which he resolved to devote the remainder of his life. After Sophie's premature and painful death from tuberculosis in 1797, Novalis experienced an overpowering vision of her presence while contemplating her grave; this is recorded in his journal in some detail and was to provide the point of departure for his *Hymnen an die Nacht*. Just before the journal breaks off, he notes, cryptically, 'Christus und Sophie'; several of his later writings suggest that Sophie had become inseparably associated with the Saviour in his mind. During the four years by which he survived her, he remained restlessly active, compiling aphorisms (*Blütenstaub*, 1798), essays, two fragmentary novels (*Heinrich von Ofterdingen* and *Die Lehrlinge zu Sais*), and two cycles of poems (*Geistliche Lieder* and *Hymnen an die Nacht*). A champion of the spirit of true poetry against the incursions both of classical formality and soulless modernism, his attitude is perhaps best summed up in the aphorism 'Die Welt muß romantisiert werden'. This is not to be understood as a plea for alienation effects in the modern sense, as some recent critics have maintained, but as part of an attempt to relate the phenomena of this world to what Novalis took to be their spiritual origins. The role of the artist was to be that of a priest or a visionary capable of initiating his fellow men into the secrets of the universe. 'Nach Innen geht der geheimnisvolle Weg. In uns, oder nirgends ist die Ewigkeit mit ihren Welten, die Vergangenheit und Zukunft. Die Außenwelt ist die Schattenwelt', he writes in *Blütenstaub*; hence the emphasis, in all his mature works, on attaining a proper understanding of death. *Hymnen an die Nacht* culminates with an expression of longing for death, and Heinrich, the apprentice poet of the educational novel *Heinrich von Ofterdingen*, must seek liberation from the confines of his mundane existence and receive instruction in the Monastery of the Dead, which provides the subject of 'Das Lied der Toten'.

The Poems

'Klagen eines Jünglings.' Written in early 1791, published in April 1791 in Wieland's *Teutscher Merkur*. Wieland described it as 'den ersten, noch wilden aber anmutigen Gesang einer jungen Muse'. Probably the best known of approximately 300 poems composed by Novalis during his school and university days, and the only one to be printed during his lifetime, 'Klagen eines Jünglings' displays many of the qualities of its author's mature work: formal control, underlying passion, and a longing for death in the face of a life recognised as being inadequate. The first four stanzas extol the pleasures of youth, while in the last four, Novalis rejects the 'unmanly' (42) gifts which Fate has bestowed on him. The central fifth stanza serves to pinpoint the cause of this apparent change of mood: here the poet recalls the effect of 'eines edlen Dulders Seele' (38), a reference to Schiller, whose illness of January to March 1791 Novalis had observed at first hand and whose powers of endurance impressed him deeply. The result is a high-minded pledge to overcome the frivolous mood of the age. The metre is that of Schiller's poem 'Die Götter Griechenlands'.

(8) 'rebengrünen Schläfe': a pastoral conceit, and as such a fitting illustration of the decadent life from which the young man wishes to break away. Novalis uses the archaic masculine 'der Schlaf' (plural 'die Schläfe') for 'temple(s)', where modern German would require 'die Schläfe' (plural 'die Schläfen').

(11f.) The youth admits to a tendency to retreat into dreams in the face of adversity.

(15) 'Klärchen': the young man's beloved.

(20) 'Ganymeda': goddess of youth.

(25) 'Zypris': 'the Cyprian', alternative name of Aphrodite, goddess of love.

(57) 'Parze': 'Parca', a personification of Fate, depicted holding a spindle.

Further Reading. Paul Kluckhohn, 'Schillers Wirkung auf Friedrich von Hardenberg', *Euphorion* 35 (1934), pp. 507–14.

'Wer einsam sitzt in seiner Kammer.' Written spring/summer 1799, first published in *Musen-Almanach*, 1802. *Geistliche Lieder* 3. In some ways, it provides an answer to the poem 'Klagen eines Jünglings'. Immersion in the mysteries of religion offered solace to many Romantics, including Friedrich Schlegel and Brentano. The cycle *Geistliche Lieder* comprises fifteen poems written between March 1799 and September 1800 in the tradition of the Pietist hymn. Novalis's authorship is betrayed by references to the death of his beloved, which is presented as a parallel to Christ's work of salvation (21f.).

(1f.) An echo of Goethe's poem 'Wer nie sein Brot mit Tränen aß'.

(11) 'Schloß': the 'lock' or 'seal' on the book of history, denying man access to the past.

(25–9) 'Lieb', 'Arme', 'Blut': Novalis follows the Pietist tradition of dwelling on the physical manifestations of Christ's love and sacrifice.

Further Reading. Margot Seidel, *Die geistlichen Lieder des Novalis und ihre Stellung zum Kirchenlied.* Diss., Bonn, 1973.

'Ich sehe dich in tausend Bildern.' Written early 1800, first published in *Novalis Schriften*, 1802. *Geistliche Lieder* 15. The intensely personal nature of religious experience is reflected by the poet's rejection of the thousands of visual depictions of the Virgin Mary. The image he retains of her in his mind inevitably surpasses the work of all artists (1) and, indeed, all other experiences (5f.). Novalis departs from Protestant orthodoxy by focusing on the Virgin Mary in what is usually taken to be the last hymn of the cycle.

(7) 'ein unnennbar süßer Himmel': Novalis deliberately used hackneyed expressions ('durch den Gebrauch ausgespielte Worte', as he calls them), which, for the modern reader, may possess a cloying effect. He believed that there was much to be gained from such indeterminate words as 'süß', 'warm', 'mild', and 'lieblich', which, because of their ambivalence, could trigger off many different associations in the reader's mind; compare the following aphorism: 'Dem Dichter ist die Sprache nie zu arm. . .Seine Welt ist einfach, wie sein Instrument — aber ebenso unerschöpflich an Melodien'.

Further Reading. Iring Fetscher, 'Eros und Religiosität', in Marcel Reich-Ranicki (ed.), *Frankfurter Anthologie*, vol. 2, Frankfurt, 1977, pp. 30f.

'Lied des Einsiedlers.' Written early 1800, first published in *Heinrich von Ofterdingen*, 1802. Recited by one of Heinrich's spiritual mentors, a hermit, in Chapter 5 of the novel. Like the pilgrim, the hermit was a stock figure in Romantic poetry. Content with his transitory earthly existence, he expresses himself in biblical images — 'Tale' ('vale') and 'Ton' ('clay'). Again, there are noticeable deviations from Christian orthodoxy. The hermit believes himself to have arrived at heaven's gate

(7f.) and to be transfigured (13–16) while still on earth; there is no mention of God, and the Virgin again occupies a central position (11f.).

(3) 'Der Liebe volle Schale': the eucharist.

(14) 'schlechten': here probably used in the archaic sense of 'schlicht' ('simple').

Further Reading. Johannes Mahr, *Übergang zum Endlichen. Der Weg des Dichters in Novalis' "Heinrich von Ofterdingen"*, Munich, 1970, pp. 142–4.

'Wenn nicht mehr Zahlen und Figuren.' Written in 1800 for the second part of *Heinrich von Ofterdingen*, and first published in an emended form in Tieck's *Bericht über die Fortsetzung*, with the comment: 'In folgendem Gedichte. . .hat der Verfasser auf die leichteste Weise den innern Geist seiner Bücher ausgedrückt'. For the original wording, see Kluckhohn and Samuel, I, pp. 344f. The poem expresses with great concision Novalis's yearning for a new age of poetic intuition in which mere 'scientific' data will no longer be heeded, and minstrels and lovers will achieve a profounder understanding of Nature than the wisest of scholars. Apparent oppositions ('Welt'/'Leben', 'Licht'/'Schatten') will be overcome, and fables and poems will replace factual chronicles. The importance attached by Novalis and many other Romantics to the *Märchen* shines through here. How does he propose to attain his Utopia? Not by a long evolutionary process, but by means of a single, magical formula, which Heinrich, the poet-priest hero of the novel, has yet to discover. Compare Eichendorff's 'Wünschelrute'.

(5f.) 'Welt': here used negatively, like 'Erdgeist' in the following poem.

Further Reading. For an exhaustive analysis of the poet's Utopian aspirations, see Hans-Joachim Mähl, *Die Idee des goldenen Zeitalters im Werk des Novalis*, Heidelberg, 1965.

'Das Lied der Toten.' Written in 1800, first published in 1802 (see previous poem). Schrimpf describes it as 'vielleicht das vollendetste und in sich geschlossenste Gedicht der deutschen Frühromantik'. The text of the cluttered four-page manuscript bears the heading 'Selig sind allein die Todten'. It was repeatedly revised, and Novalis seems to have rearranged the order of the stanzas several times. Tieck's version is here reproduced, bar the misprint in line 8. The poem constitutes an inscription in the churchyard of the Monastery of the Dead, where Heinrich von Ofterdingen was to have learnt the true meaning of death, man's spiritual home in Novalis's philosophy. The dead are thought of as lacking nothing (stanza 2), they have no cause to weep or lament (stanza 4), and no cloud or wind mars their tranquil existence (stanza 5). They know the secret of love (stanzas 7–10) and are part of the great ocean of life (stanzas 6 and 12). They appeal to those who have died recently to cast off the trappings of their earthly existence and join them (stanza 13). If only men knew the joys that await them, they would willingly surrender their lives (stanza 14), and the evil 'Erdgeist' would be banished (stanza 15). Stanza 7, which introduces the theme of elemental love, occupies a central position and differs from the rest of the poem in that the rhymes are identical. The emphasis on the pleasures of the hereafter is explained by a line from *Blütenstaub*: 'Wir werden mehr genießen als je, denn unser Geist hat entbehrt'.

(7f.) A steady stream of newcomers bring warmth to the spacious hearths of the Monastery. Tieck emended 'frische' to 'neue', for unknown reasons.

(45–8) Water imagery is here, as often in Pietist writings, associated with God, the 'fountainhead' of life. Compare lines 88–96.

(49) The comma emphasises 'Liebe': 'Only now has *love* become our life.'

(77) 'Hügel': '[burial] mound'.

(81–8) The sorrowful memory may be of the crucifixion, linked, as ever, with Sophie's death.

(96) 'Wirbel': two meanings are suggested by this ambiguous term — 'vertebrae' and 'whirlpools', the former providing a link with the physical, the latter with the liquid images.

(113, 120) 'Erdgeist': a term probably borrowed from Goethe's *Faust*, but here employed in a less positive sense as the spirit of a modern, utilitarian world, inferior to the rich and fulfilling existence of the dead.

Further Reading. Hans–Joachim Schrimpf, 'Novalis. Das Lied der Toten', in Benno von Wiese (ed.), *Die Deutsche Lyrik*, Düsseldorf, 1956, pp. 414–29; Paul Kluckhohn, 'Neue Funde zu Friedrich von Hardenbergs (Novalis) Arbeit am "Heinrich von Ofterdingen"', *Deutsche Vierteljahrsschrift für Literaturwissenschaft und Geistesgeschichte* 32 (1958), pp. 319–409.

Clemens Brentano

Editions

Clemens Brentano. *Sämtliche Werke und Briefe. Historisch–kritische Ausgabe.* Veranstaltet vom Freien Deutschen Hochstift. Edited by Jürgen Behrens, Wolfgang Frühwald, and Detlev Lüders, Stuttgart, 1975– (in progress).

Clemens Brentano. *Werke.* Edited by Wolfgang Frühwald, Bernhard Gajek, and Friedhelm Kemp, 4 vols., Munich, 1968, 2nd ed. 1978.

General Reading

Wolfgang Pfeiffer–Belli, *Clemens Brentano,* Freiburg, 1947.

Werner Hoffmann, *Clemens Brentano. Leben und Werk,* Munich, 1966.

John J. Fetzer, *Romantic Orpheus. Profiles of Clemens Brentano,* Berkeley, 1974.

Walter Müller–Seidel, 'Brentanos naive und sentimentalische Poesie', *Jahrbuch der Deutschen Schillergesellschaft* 18 (1974), pp. 441–65.

Erika Tunner, *Clemens Brentano (1778–1842). Imagination et sentiment religieux,* 2 vols., Paris, 1977.

John J. Fetzer, *Clemens Brentano,* Boston, 1981.

Wolfgang Frühwald, 'Clemens Brentano', in Benno von Wiese (ed.), *Deutsche Dichter der Romantik,* Berlin, 1983, pp. 344–76.

Brigitte Schad, *Quellenverwandlung beim frühen Brentano,* Frankfurt, 1983.

Helene M. Kastinger Riley, *Clemens Brentano,* Stuttgart, 1985.

Life

Widely regarded as the 'most fascinating and the most ambiguous of the Romantics' (Pfeiffer-Belli), Clemens Maria Wenzeslaus Brentano was descended from an ancient Italian family that had been established in Frankfurt for several generations. His father married three times and had a total of twenty children; his mother, the daughter of the novelist Sophie von La Roche, bore her husband twelve of these and died in childbirth at the age of 37. Clemens was dispatched to live with an aunt and then to Winterwerber's supposedly enlightened boarding school in Mannheim, the 'Kurpfälzisches Erziehungsinstitut für Zöglinge des männlichen Geschlechts aller drei christlichen Religionsparteien'. At the University of Bonn, which he entered as a student of mineralogy, he acquired a reputation for his collections of pipes and colourful clothes. He certainly lacked the acumen of a businessman, the career his father chose for him, and repeatedly proved himself incapable of grasping the essentials of a practical career. Some critics would see in his life-long hostility to the bourgeois and the philistine a reaction against his father, who evinced little affection for him during his childhood. The quest for a mother-figure is a recurring theme in his works.

After transferring to the University of Jena in 1798, he began to move among the early Romantics, meeting August Schlegel, Schelling and Tieck. Classical ideals of harmony and serenity were alien to him: for most of his life, Brentano was to see himself as melancholic, misunderstood by the world, and torn by inner conflicts. His friends referred to him not as 'Clemens', but as 'Demens'. From the turn of the century onwards, he produced a variety of poetic works in quick succession, poems, several plays, and a two-volume novel with the strange title *Godwi oder das steinerne Bild der Mutter. Ein verwilderter Roman von Maria* (1801). Written in a mixture of prose and verse, it contains some of the best-known poems of German Romanticism. But the atmosphere of mystery that was carefully built up in the first part of the novel is relentlessly destroyed in the second, when the author meets some of his fictional characters and comments derisively on them. Already Brentano was becoming aware of the limitations of the movement and experimenting with methods of ironising and deflating the fantasy world of the early Romantics. 'Romantic irony' was to become a major characteristic of early nineteenth-century poetry.

It could be argued that Brentano's most enduring contribution to German literature was the famous anthology of folk poetry *Des Knaben Wunderhorn*, edited in collaboration with Achim von Arnim between 1805 and 1808. The three years of his marriage to Sophie Mereau — a divorced Protestant eight years older than himself — were probably the happiest in his life, although none of the three children she bore him survived, and she herself died in childbirth in 1806. Alone again, Brentano saw himself as a galley slave ('der Galeerensklave vom toten Meere'), and fluctuated between periods of rakish debauchery, sombre introspection and frenetic creative work. His second marriage, to Auguste Bußmann, was of short duration, owing to their incompatibility, and from this point onwards Brentano's poetry becomes increasingly personal and confessional; in it, religious imagery intertwines with references to unwholesome sensual experiences. These tensions are finally resolved by Brentano's religious crisis of 1815, after which the poet

[108]

seems determined to regain the lost faith of his youth. His relationship with Louise Hensel ended in renunciation in 1817, and shortly thereafter the poet set off for Dülmen in Westphalia, where he spent five years at the bedside of the stigmatised nun Anna Katharina Emmerick, noting down her visions and transports in eleven manuscript volumes. Only one of these was published during his lifetime. After her death in 1824, he continued working for Catholic causes, producing a few *Märchen* and numerous half-factual, half-visionary writings, many of which still await publication. There can be no definitive version of Brentano's poems. Most of them were repeatedly reworked by the author, only to be revised by his brother Christian, the first editor of his collected works.

The Poems

'Lore Lay.' Written 1799, published in *Godwi*, vol. 2, chap. 36, where it is sung by Violetta. Brentano claims to have invented the Rhine maiden, giving her the name of a dangerous rock situated on the right bank of the river near Bacharach and famous for its echo. In older sources such as Freher's *Origines Palatinae* of 1612, there is mention of a 'Lurleberg' endowed with an echo formerly attributed to water sprites or dwarfs. Brentano's Lore Lay is a sorceress interrogated by a bishop who falls in love with her. She is dispatched to a convent, but begs the three knights who are accompanying her to let her take one last look at the river and at her unfaithful lover's castle. Claiming to see her beloved in a ship, she hurls herself into the Rhine, leaving the knights marooned on a rock subsequently known as the 'Dreiritterstein'. In another version of this poem, the passenger in the ship is the bishop himself.

(17–24) Lore Lay is well aware of the power she has over men and asks the bishop to put her to death.

(24, 29) 'Stab': the only 'magic wand' she possesses is her own body.

(41–56) The woman relates her demonic powers to her lover's deceitfulness.

(88, 90) 'Der soll', 'Er muß': the traveller's identity remains uncertain.

(101–03) The repetition reproduces the triple echo of the cliff.

Further Reading. Willy Krogmann, 'Lorelei. Geburt einer Sage', *Rheinisch-Westfälische Zeitschrift für Volkskunde* 3 (1956), pp. 170–96; Klaus-Dieter Krabiel, 'Die beiden Fassungen von Brentanos "Lureley"' *Literaturwissenschaftliches Jahrbuch der Görres–Gesellschaft* 6 (1965), pp. 128–31; Schad, *Quellenverwandlung*, pp. 21–52. See also Heine, 'Ich weiß nicht, was soll es bedeuten', below.

'Großmutter Schlangenköchin.' Published in *Godwi*, vol. 2, chap. 14, where the author recalls singing it with his sister as a child; the individual couplets are headed alternately 'Mutter' and 'Kind'. In a letter of 1806, Brentano claims to have heard it from an 80-year-old Swabian woman. It was given its title and reprinted with minor variations in *Des Knaben Wunderhorn* (I, 19). The relentless question-and-answer structure recalls a forensic trial, except that no conclusion is reached. The main circumstances of the tragedy are left to the imagination. The poem's apparent simplicity gives it the direct, moving effect which the Romantics wished to achieve. Monotonous repetitions increase the sense of suspense. The mother's apparently tranquil acceptance of the death of her only child may imply a degree of complicity in the events. Brentano's contemporaries were impressed; Goethe praised it as 'Tief, rätselhaft, dramatisch vortrefflich behandelt'.

    (1)   'zur Stube': 'for dinner'.

    (15) the 'Fischlein' turns out to have been a venomous snake.

Further Reading. 'Die Schlangenköchin', in *Deutsche Volkslieder und ihre Melodien*, vol. 4, pt. 4, edited by Erich Seemann and Walter Wiora, Berlin, 1959, pp. 189–215; Schad, *Quellenverwandlung*, pp. 66–92.

'Der Spinnerin Nachtlied.' Written in 1802, published in Brentano's *Chronika eines fahrenden Schülers*, in Friedrich Förster's *Die Sängerfahrt*, 1818. Several manuscript versions exist, but the now current title 'Der Spinnerin Lied' derives from the posthumous edition. The poem is one of Brentano's most popular. Again, the apparent simplicity of this poetic monologue in the style of a folk song conceals an elaborate structure, in which the few haunting rhymes and assonances illustrate both the woman's repetitive work and her cyclic thought processes. We search in vain for a rational investigation of the attendant circumstances of her misfortune. The poem has been construed as a lament for 'a remote past, a paradise that may be recalled but not regained' (Fetzer). The identical lines 16 and 21, however, imply a return to harmony through death and so reflect a spiritual affinity with early Romanticism. The final stanza, with its four self-contained paratactic clauses, slows the rhythm down and points towards the fulfilment of the spinner's wishes.

    (12, 17) 'gefahren': the context suggests 'passed away' rather than 'travelled'.

    (16, 21) 'wolle': 'may He' (if He wishes).

Further Reading. S. S. Prawer, 'Der Spinnerin Lied', in idem, *German Lyric Poetry*, London, 1952, pp. 121–6; Richard Alewyn, 'Clemens Brentano — Der Spinnerin Lied', *Wirkendes Wort* 11 (1961), pp. 45–7; Lida Kirchberger, 'Der Spinnerin Lied: A Fresh Appraisal', *Monatshefte* 67 (1975), pp. 417–24; Wolfgang Frühwald, 'Die artistische Konstruktion des Volkstones. Zu Clemens Brentanos *Der Spinnerin Nachtlied*', in Wulf Segebrecht (ed.), *Gedichte und Interpretationen III: Klassik und Romantik*, Stuttgart, 1984, pp. 269–79.

'Die Welt war mir zuwider.' Written *c.* 1812, published posthumously in vol. II of *Clemens Brentanos Gesammelte Schriften*, 1852–5. Often referred to by its refrain, 'O lieb Mädel, wie schlecht bist du!', this poem is one of Brentano's most striking creations. As in 'Großmutter Schlangenköchin', the central paradox is that of a 'dear' woman's wickedness. In simple, four-line stanzas followed by an unchanging refrain, Brentano describes a relationship with a woman of easy virtue. The humiliations attendant on this courtship are vividly evoked: the waiting at street corners, the mockery of his friends and, eventually, the deadly poison with which she infects him. A case study of a self-destroying passion, the poem embodies the Romantic's yearning for the impossible no less than it expresses his latent propensity towards disease and death. Rarely has the contrast between innocence and sin, between spiritual purity and sensual depravity, been made in more direct and moving tones.

(18) 'Daß dich mein Lieben rühre': in the hope that my love would move you'.

(38f.) The disease is used in its literal sense and also as a metaphor for a deeper, spiritual malaise.

'Frühlingsschrei eines Knechtes aus der Tiefe.' Written in the spring of 1816, shortly before Brentano became acquainted with Louise Hensel, published in Heinrich Kletke (ed.), *Geistliche Blumenlese aus deutschen Dichtern von Novalis bis auf die Gegenwart*, 1841, as 'Erbarme dich, Herr!'. One copy was sent to Louise with the explanation: 'Damit sie aber einen Begriff habe, wie es mir in der Einsamkeit des Herzens zumute ist . . .'. The title harbours another paradoxical formulation: the season of spring produces a cry, as if of pain. Brentano's 'Knecht' represents man as he is often portrayed in the Bible, as the 'servant' of God, while the 'depths' recall the opening verse of Psalm 130 ('Aus der Tiefe rufe ich, Herr, zu dir'). The ever-present threat of drowning is a reminiscence of the biblical Flood, and there are noteworthy correspondences with the water imagery in Psalm 69 ('Gott, hilf mir; denn das Wasser geht mir bis an die Seele'); cf. especially lines 2–4 and 15f. The advent of spring affects the poet in this manner partly because it is the season of melting snow, and partly because it marks the return of yet another year of futile labour. 'Der Frühling ist die Figur der hoffnungslosen Wiederkehr des immer Gleichen', comments Curt Hohoff. The setting is realistically portrayed: the poet envisages himself as a labourer cleaning out an underground well. The shaft is unstable (24) and threatens to collapse on him and bury him alive. The more frantically he strives, the greater the danger. But there are poignant hints that the well is also inside himself: the water represents the poison that is within him. The poem builds up to a crescendo of increasing terror, as the well becomes more constricted and the servant senses that he cannot accomplish his task unaided (stanzas 12–14). He realises that his screams are further examples of his arrogance. Only in the final stanza does the direct appeal to Chirst hold out a promise of help. The feminine rhymes have a gently lilting effect which softens the otherwise uncompromising tone of the poem.

(1) 'Meister': one of several images that work on two levels — the labourer is calling his master as the poet is calling on his Lord.

(2) 'Abgrund': 'abyss', in a physical and in a spiritual sense.

(4) 'Lichte': the contrast between light and darkness is made repeatedly.

(6) 'Erde', 'Herzen': the analogy between outer and inner reality is particularly obvious in this parallelism.

(19) 'lauert': spring is envisaged as a hostile force, a beast of prey waiting for an opportunity to pounce.

(28) 'Fluch', 'Witz': neither curses nor imaginative reasoning can help.

(32) 'Sündflut': a pun on 'Sintflut' ('Great Flood').

(34f.) 'Lämmer', 'Früchte': the poet appears now to be rejecting both his personal acquaintances, the 'lambs' he used to greet, and his poetic works, the 'fruits' he cultivated.

(39f.) Another expression of the poet's outcast state: 'Not one of earth's springtimes ever had mercy on me'.

(51) 'arbeitblut'gen': 'bloody from my labours'.

(56) 'Regenbogen': cf. Genesis 9:13ff.

(58–60) 'I heard it said when I was young that Your blood possessed, ah, wondrous powers of salvation'.

Further Reading. Harry Tucker, 'Clemens Brentano: The Imagery of

Despair and Salvation', *Modern Language Quarterly* 14 (1953), pp. 284–97; Curt Hohoff and Anneliese de Haas, 'Clemens Brentano: *Frühlingsschrei eines Knechtes aus der Tiefe'*, in Rupert Hirschenauer and Albrecht Weber (eds.), *Wege zum Gedicht*, Munich, 1956, pp. 199–207; Wolfgang Frühwald, 'Der Bergmann in der Seele Schacht. Zu Clemens Brentanos Gedicht *Frühlingsschrei eines Knechtes aus der Tiefe'*, in Wulf Segebrecht (ed.), *Gedichte und Interpretationen III: Klassik und Romantik*, Stuttgart, 1984, pp. 437–50.

'Wenn der lahme Weber träumt, er webe.' Published in the second edition of *Das Märchen von Gockel, Hinkel und Gackeleia*, 1838. The first half of the poem takes the form of a catalogue of dreams or delusions on the part of an assortment of handicapped individuals, creatures, or objects ('Weber', 'Lerche', 'Nachtigall', 'Erz', 'Eisenherz'). Even abstract qualities ('Nüchternheit') partake of this yearning for fulfilment. After the semicolon in line 10, the atmosphere of quiet, pathetic nostalgia is destroyed by the arrival of 'naked truth', and the dreams are dispelled by the glaring lights and shrill noises of reality. Internal rhymes proliferate, threatening to obscure the meaning of certain lines (9f.), as does the personification of abstract concepts. The theme is the clash between dreams and reality, Romanticism and Realism, and in this conflict the powers of the imagination must eventually succumb to the truth. The limits of the Romantic imagination are explored, as they were by most of the later poets of the movement.

(4) 'des Widerhalls': 'at the sound of the reverberation' (of her singing).

(6) 'der drei je zählte kaum': 'he who could hardly count up to three ' (proverbial).

(10) 'shyness intoxicating itself with wine'.

(14) 'übern Haufen (rennen)': to run down, demolish (colloquial).

(15) 'Schmerz-Schalmeien': sound and feeling are brought together in this unusual example of synaesthesia ('shawms of pain').

Further Reading. Hans Magnus Enzensberger, *Brentanos Poetik*. Munich, 1961, repr. 1973, pp. 34–56.

Adelbert von Chamisso

Editions

Adelbert von Chamisso. Sämtliche Werke. Edited by Jost Perfahl and Volker Hoffman, 2 vols., Munich, 1975.

Adelbert von Chamisso. Sämtliche Werke. Edited by Werner Feudel and Christel Laufer, 2 vols., Leipzig, 1980, repr. Munich, 1982.

General Reading

Elisabeth Ehrlich, *Das französische Element in der Lyrik Chamissos*, Berlin, 1932, repr. 1967.

Doerte Brockhagen, 'Adelbert von Chamisso', in Alberto Martino (ed.), *Literatur in der sozialen Bewegung. Aufsätze und Forschungsberichte zum 19. Jahrhundert*, Tübingen, 1977, pp. 373–423.

Werner Feudel, *Adelbert von Chamisso. Leben und Werk*, 2nd ed., Leipzig, 1980.

Dorothea von Chamisso, *Adelbert von Chamisso: Bild seines Lebens.* Berlin, 1980.

Peter A. Kroner, 'Adelbert von Chamisso', in Benno von Wiese (ed.), *Deutsche Dichter der Romantik*, Berlin, 1983, pp. 439–58.

Peter Lahnstein, *Adelbert von Chamisso. Der Preuße aus Frankreich*, Munich, 1984.

Life

Born Louis Charles Adelaide Chamisso, the man we now know as Adelbert von Chamisso was the son of a French count forced into exile by the French Revolution. His ancestral home, the castle of Boncourt in Champagne, was eventually razed to the ground in 1793. For many years the Chamisso family lived in straitened circumstances. When they arrived in Berlin their lot improved somewhat, and Adelbert became a page-boy to the Queen of Prussia, briefly attended the Collège Français, and then entered the Prussian army. Like Brentano, but for different reasons, he was acutely conscious of being an outcast both in France and in Germany. It was not until 1812 that he finally decided to make Germany his permanent home. Under the influence of Novalis and August Schlegel, he began writing *Märchen*, although by the second decade of the nineteenth century he had also resolved to devote himself to the study of medicine and botany. His highly successful short prose narrative, *Peter Schlemihls wundersame Geschichte*, an allegori-

[114]

cal tale of a man who sells his shadow, was published in 1814.

Many of the Romantics were keen travellers, but Chamisso was the only poet among them to sail round the world. In 1815, he joined a scientific expedition financed by a wealthy Russian with the aim of seeking the North-East Passage from the Pacific to the Atlantic. He was absent for nearly four years, and although the *Rurik* under Captain Otto von Kotzebue did not get further than the west coast of Alaska, the journey took in many tropical islands in the Pacific and enabled Chamisso to collect and classify some 2,500 new specimens of plant life and to study the life of the island people at first hand. Here, too, he could live out his vision of himself as a restless, uprooted wanderer. Observing the people he encountered, he concluded that most tribes had already been corrupted by traders and missionaries, but he provides an interesting first-hand account of some uncontacted islanders, especially one Kadu from Radack, in his written account of the journey.

After his return to Germany, his life became more settled: he married and, following in Peter Schlemihl's footsteps, worked as a botanist in Berlin. His first collection of verse appeared in 1827, from which time on he gradually established his reputation as a clear-sighted and humorous observer and critic of his times. Lyric poems extolling the beauties of Nature are rare, as are subjective religious or philosophical confessions. 'Jedem Liede müßte als Novelle die Begebenheit nacherzählt werden können', he writes, and his poems are not outpourings of the soul in the manner of Novalis and Brentano, but stories that have been put together with meticulous care. Although he continues to derive inspiration from ancient lays and chronicles, a new note of realism makes itself felt in much of Chamisso's work. Literature and scholarship kept him equally occupied to the end of his life. He edited several editions of the influential periodical *Deutscher Musenalmanach*, and published numerous scientific papers as well as a vivid description of his travels, *Reise um die Welt* (1836). For all his involvement in the cultural life of Germany, he never lost his French accent, and during the last days of the feverish illness to which he succumbed in 1838, he is said to have communicated solely in his native tongue.

The Poems

'Das Schloß Boncourt.' Written in 1827, published in *Berliner Conversations-Blatt*, 1827. Chamisso had seen the site of his family's historic seat in the course of his travels in France in 1807, and mentions the profound effect of the visit in a letter to Xavier Marnier in 1836. The poem focuses on an experience of central importance to the exile: how to come to terms with the loss of his home and the deterioration of his personal circumstances. The answer, as it is here given, is through an active acceptance of the present, exemplified by the anonymous plough-man who receives the poet's blessing in stanza 8. The poem begins as a dream, but the initial vision is soon superseded by a sober recognition of the inevitable, reinforced by the reassuring knowledge that the ground on which the castle once stood is providing others with work and sustenance.

(6f.) 'schimmerndes. . .kenne': the vision slowly takes shape.

(10) 'Löwen': lions were depicted on Chamisso's coat of arms.

(21) 'umflort': 'blurred'.

'Der Invalid im Irrenhaus.' Written in 1827, published in an appendix to the second edition of *Peter Schlemihl*, 1827. Several poets took up the theme of the injustices done to war veterans (Uhland, 'Am 18. Oktober 1816'; Heine, 'Der Tambourmajor'), but Chamisso's poem has wider implications: the value of the Wars of Liberation is questioned; that the people are no better off afterwards is indicated by the 'Grimm'ge Wächter' of stanzas 4 and 5. The concept of freedom is itself shown to be relative: here, the soldier is less free than he was before his campaign, and Chamisso may well have felt this to be true of the position of the individual in the majority of the German states after the Congress of Vienna, and especially after the repressive Carlsbad Decrees of 1819.

(1) 'Leipzig': site of the Battle of the Nations, 16–19 October 1813, in which the combined German armies inflicted a decisive defeat on Napoleon.

(2) 'Schmach für Unbill': 'injury turned into disgrace'.

(3) 'Freiheit!': Field-Marshall Blücher's rallying-call.

(6) 'Was ein Tor. . .': a clear indication of Chamisso's disillusionment about the objectives of the war.

'Das Riesen-Spielzeug.' Written in September 1831, published in *Deutscher Musenalmanach*, 1833. Written in a modified form of the 'Nibelungenstrophe' and thus metrically similar to the medieval 'Lay of the Nibelungs', this poem is the first of a short cycle entitled 'Deutsche Volkssagen', and was directly inspired by Grimm's compendium of *Deutsche Sagen*, which contains a very similar prose account of the story (no. 15). The main difference, typical of Chamisso, is that a connection is made in the final stanza between the young girl's wanton treatment of the peasantry and the eventual disapperance of the giants. This suggests, in political terms, that the aristocracy are doomed if they use the rural population as mere playthings: the cause of the French Revolution is here paraphrased *in nuce*.

(1) 'Burg Niedeck': the ruins of this vast castle are still to be seen in the Vosges mountains near Oberhaslach (see line 10).

(5) 'Riesen-Fräulein': '[noble] daughter of the giants'; 'Fräulein' originally denoted noble birth.

(6) 'sonder Wartung': 'unattended'.

(14) 'baut': 'cultivates' (hence 'Bauer').

(27) 'Zappliges': 'creepy-crawly' (quoted from Grimm).

(34) 'kein Spielzeug nicht': emphatic double negative ('definitely not a toy').

Further Reading. Valerie Höttges, *Die Sage vom Riesenspielzeug*, Jena, 1931; Friedrich Ranke, 'Das Riesenspielzeug', *Volkssage* (1934), pp. 39–51.

'Die Weiber von Winsperg.' Written in October 1831, posthumously published in *Werke*, 1852. Chamisso's immediate source was, again, Grimm's *Deutsche Sagen* (no. 493); the tale ultimately derives from the Cologne *Kaiserchronik* of 1175. In Grimm, the women set out to trick the king by making the surrender of Winsperg conditional on their being allowed to take with them as much as they can carry. Here, however, the monarch invites them to do so, apparently without any prompting on their part. Chamisso also stresses the 'blocking' function of the chancellor; the king overrules him in this instance, but it is implied that modern heads of state are less scrupulous in observing their commitments to the people.

(1) 'Konrad': Konrad III (1138–52).

(2) 'Winsperg': small town in Swabia (Weinsberg near Heilbronn).

(3) 'Der Welfe': 'the Guelph', Duke Heinrich of Bavaria, supported by the townspeople.

(7) 'Degen': 'warrior'.

(19) 'bedrängte': 'besieged'.

(28) 'zerdeutet und zerdreht': 'reinterpreted and twisted' (by hair-splitting arguments).

Further Reading. Friedrich Ranke, 'Die Weiber von Weinsberg', *Volkssage* (1934), pp. 5–21; K. Weller, 'Die neuere Forschung von den treuen Weinsberger Weibern', *Zeitschrift für württembergische Landesgeschichte* 4 (1940), pp. 1–17.

'Das Dampfroß.' Written in 1830, published in *Berliner Musenalmanach*, 1831. One of the earliest poems in German on the potential consequences of railway travel. Although Chamisso took a more positive view of this development than many of his contemporaries, this poem portrays the crankish inventor of a 'steam horse' who claims that, by travelling at top speed from east to west, he will be able to outrun the sun and arrive at his starting point before he departed. Various humorous situations follow on from this basic idea.

(27) 'zu eifern geneigt': 'inclined to be jealous'. He clearly did not welcome his grandson's presence at his wedding.

(41–6) The blacksmith belatedly tries to obtain some useful information about potential investments.

(47) 'Feder': 'spring', 'throttle'.

'Pech.' Written in 1828, published in Schütze's *Taschenbuch für das Jahr 1831*. One of many poems on a set character, the 'Pechvogel' or 'bird of ill-luck', a type much mocked in early nineteenth-century literature. Here, the unlucky fellow defends himself by recounting situations in which he 'almost made it'. Not the least of the poem's themes is the social division between rich and poor (stanza 5), aristocrat and bourgeois (stanzas 6f.).

(8) 'War ich aber nicht der Tor': 'I wasn't such a fool as to. . .'.

Des Knaben Wunderhorn

Editions

Clemens Brentano: Sämtliche Werke und Briefe. Historisch-kritische Ausgabe,
Veranstaltet vom Freien Deutschen Hochstift. Vols. 6–9, 3, edited by
Heinz Rölleke, Stuttgart, 1975–8.

Des Knaben Wunderhorn, Edited by Willi Koch, Munich, 1957.

Des Knaben Wunderhorn, Edited by Arthur Henkel, 3 vols., Munich,
1963.

General Reading

John Meier, *Kunstlieder im Volksmund.* Leipzig, 1906, repr. Hildesheim, 1976.

Karl Bode, *Die Bearbeitung der Vorlagen in Des Knaben Wunderhorn,*
Berlin, 1909.

Max Kommerell, *Das Volkslied und das deutsche Lied,* Marburg, 1936.

Vladimir Karbusicky, *Ideologie im Lied — Lied in der Ideologie,* Cologne,
1972.

Ernst Klusen, *Volkslied. Fund und Erfindung,* Cologne, 1969.

Wolfgang Suppan, *Volkslied,* Stuttgart, 1965.

Hermann Strobach, 'Herders Volksliedbegriff. Geschichtliche und
gegenwärtige Bedeutung', *Jahrbuch für Volkskunde und Kulturgeschichte*
6 (1978), pp. 9–55.

Origins and Genesis

Interest in the so-called 'folk song' dates from the middle of the
eighteenth century. One of the first serious attempts to collect and
publish the popular verse of the past was undertaken in England by
Thomas Percy (*Reliques of Ancient English Poetry,* 1765). This anthology
contained romances and informal ballads as well as sonnets and material
from early manuscript sources. Percy's work did much to stimulate
interest in early English poems and in Nordic and Celtic traditions. James
Macpherson's editions of Scottish verse, notably the counterfeit
epics he ascribed to the poet Ossian, which also appeared in the 1760s,
helped to generate enthusiasm for what was taken to be the intuitive
visionary powers of the ancient bards. Goethe and his contemporaries
were impressed; it was only after Macpherson's death in 1796 that
many of the poems were shown to be forgeries. Herder was instrumental in publicising folk poetry in Germany; his collections of *Volkslieder*

(1778–9) contained contributions from many parts of the world, and in his essays he argued that the greatest poetry was produced by those minds who were in closest touch with Nature: these included the authors of the poetic sections of the Bible, Homer and Shakespeare, as well as the anonymous originators of popular verse. It was he who coined the term 'Volkslied'. In the following years, many attempts were made to collect and publish poems that circulated orally in the regions of Germany, and to rescue from oblivion those works of merit that the anthologisers encountered in ancient manuscripts, broadsheets, and early books of verse. One such attempt was Rudolph Zacharias Becker's *Mildheimisches Liederbuch* of 1799, which enjoyed some popularity at the turn of the nineteenth century, but which Achim von Arnim and Clemens Brentano found disappointing ('platt, unendlich gemein'). Together they undertook to produce a better collection, in the belief that it would convince the world of the superiority of the 'naive' oral traditions of Germany. 'Das einfache naive Volkslied ist Anfang der Poesie und Vollendung der Kunst' (August Stephan Winkelmann, 1803) is a sentiment echoed repeatedly at the time. Both editors saw themselves as educators and as defenders of the spirit against the symptoms of decadence and philistinism in the world around them.

Yet there were many minor disagreements between them on questions of editorial policy. Brentano had hoped to structure the volume in accordance with geographical principles and to devote separate sections to the various regions of Germany. Nothing came of this: Arnim, who wished to excise dialect features, transposed many of the poems into standard German and thus deprived them of their individuality. There was uncertainty as to whether they ought to follow early sources exactly, or polish them up for publication — which they frequently did. Neither of the editors had much compunction about interpolating poems of their own, or including contributions that had been sent to them with little regard for their authenticity; Brentano had, in fact, written programmatically to Arnim in 1805: 'Es muß so eingerichtet sein, daß kein Alter davon ausgeschlossen ist, es könnten die bessern Volkslieder darinne befestigt und neue hinzugedichtet werden'. It has not proved possible to distinguish between the genuine and the counterfeit in all cases, although many of the compilers' sources are available to us. Nor is it easy to assess the relative contribution of the two editors. It seems that Arnim did most of the work on the first volume, and Brentano on the second and third.

[120]

The title *Des Knaben Wunderhorn. Alte deutsche Lieder* (*The Boy's Horn of Plenty.* . . . .) was chosen by Arnim, who decided to open the anthology with a poem about a boy rider. The first volume came out in September 1805 (dated 1806), and the publishers predicted that Arnim and Brentano would outdo the English and Scottish anthologists in providing samples of what was best in each genre: 'Wir glauben durch diese Sammlung dem allgemeinen Wunsche nach näherer Kenntnis deutscher Volkslieder alles das zu gewähren, was ähnliche Sammler in Schottland und England bei viel leichterer Mitteilung kaum erreichten: eine Auswahl des besten in jeder Gattung zu liefern'. Two further volumes followed in 1808, making this by far the most substantial and broadly based collection of its kind. The three volumes comprise more than 700 poems, and most types of verse are represented — ballads, odes, hymns, nursery-rhymes, love songs, drinking songs, nonsense verse, instructive verse, lamentations, soldiers' marching songs, political lampoons, and many others.

Although Goethe, to whom the editors prudently dedicated their work, reviewed the collection favourably and generations of poets were inspired by it, there was some criticism of the editors' methods. It was soon recognised that Arnim and Brentano had used their 'edition' as a platform for some of their own work and that of their friends. Unlike the more scrupulous and disciplined Grimm brothers, Arnim and Brentano saw their compilation not as a museum of antiquities, but as a means of breathing fresh life into the poetry of their age. But not a few of their readers objected to the way they had retouched the ancient material. Friedrich Schlegel lamented, 'Wenn auch nur die Sorgfalt der Behandlung und der Auswahl dem Reichtum einigermaßen entspräche! Wenn nur nicht so manches Schlechte mit aufgenommen, so manches Eigne und fremdartige eingemischt wäre, und die bei einigen Liedern sichtbare willkürliche Veränderung nicht bei dem größten Teil der Leser ein gerechtes Mißtrauen auch gegen die übrigen einflößen müßte'. But Goethe resisted the modern demand for factual accuracy and defended the poetic truth of the compilation, stating that the original genius of folk poetry is eroded by constant recitation and thus needs to be restored by men of talent: 'Das wahre dichterische Genie, wo es auftritt, ist in sich vollendet, mag ihm Unvollkommenheit der Sprache, der äußeren Technik, oder was sonst will, entgegenstehen, es besitzt die höhere innere Form, der doch am Ende alles zu Gebote steht'. Thus what began as a great melting-pot came to be viewed as a mosaic of the German soul: 'Dieses Buch kann ich nicht genug rühmen, es enthält die holdseligsten Blüten des deutschen Geistes, und wer das deutsche Volk von einer liebenswürdigen Seite kennen lernen will, der lese diese Volkslieder' (Heine).

In the more recent past, several attempts have been made to de-mythologise the folk song. Herder's terminology was first questioned by John Meier (*Kunstlieder im Volksmund*, 1906), who argued that the poems we think of as 'folk songs' were the product of individuals rather than of the broad masses, as the word would seem to suggest. But the term will survive, if only because it is now very widely used, and there seems to be no readily acceptable alternative.

In view of the orginal editors' inconsistency in matters of presentation, I have modernized the punctuation of the *Wunderhorn* poems to a greater extent than I have done elsewhere in this edition. Bracketed numerals in the notes refer to the standard edition.

The Poems

'Der Rattenfänger von Hameln' (I, 44). This famous legend owes its origins to a stained-glass window in the Marktkirche at Hamelin, depicting the exodus of a group of citizens from the town in the thirteenth century. The picture was later re-interpreted as portraying the revenge of a disaffected rat-catcher, the 'Pied Piper' of Robert Browning's poem. There are several versions of the story; Jobst Johann Backhaus, *Chronico Hamelensis ad annum 1284* (*c*. 1590), and a poem by Samuel Erich, 'Exodus Hamelensis' (Hanover, *c*. 1660). These may have been known to Arnim; if so, he chose to depart from them in several respects. See also Grimm, *Deutsche Sagen* no. 244. The present version is obviously didactic: the solemn warnings in the first and last stanzas are addressed to careless parents rather than to dishonest councillors. The poem is in the form of a conversation between a visitor to the church (1–4) and his guide, possibly the priest or churchwarden.

  (1) 'Bilde': the picture in the church window (see above).
  (8) 'how other methods [than the use of cats] could be employed.'
  (9) 'Wundermann': 'miracle-worker', a term for a magician or sorcerer.
  (12) 'Weser': the River Weser.
  (18) 'they threatened him when he insisted angrily.
  (23) 'Betstuhl': 'pew'.
  (29–36) In *Des Knaben Wunderhorn* the children are not taken to a mountain as they are in all other versions of the story, but drowned in the river, like the rats.

[122]

Further Reading. G. C. Schmidt, 'Die Quelle des Rattenfängerlieds in *Des Knaben Wunderhorn*', *Modern Language Notes* 19 (1904), pp. 179–81; Heinrich Spanuth, *Der Rattenfänger von Hameln*, Hameln, 1951.

'Das fahrende Fräulein' (I, 114b). A characteristic mixture of ancient and modern verse. The first two stanzas derive from a book of *Frische Teutsche Liedlein* published by Georg Forster, Nuremberg, 1539; the last four are a modern invention, most probably by Arnim, in which the woman's lamentations are placed within a dramatic framework. The 'wandering courtesan' is a demonic outsider and, like Lorelei, fated to die a watery death.

(2) 'meiner Buhler Orden': 'the ranks of my lovers'.

(3) 'Nachreu': 'belated contrition'.

(15) 'dem sie nachgestellt': 'whom she used to pursue'.

'Doktor Faust' (I, 214). The text is based on a broadsheet from Cologne ('Die unglückliche Gehorsamkeit des Doktor Faust', *c.* 1763), in which the Faust legend is summarised in the rough and ready language of the popular ballad. The earliest published account of the semi-legendary black magician who sold his soul to the devil dates from 1587. It was a Lutheran tract illustrating, among other things, the futility of last-minute conversions. Several reworkings of the material were undertaken (by Christopher Marlowe and by less well-known figures) until Goethe immortalised it in his two-part drama *Faust* (1808, 1832). The present version is crude by comparison with most others.

(5) 'Anhalt': a region of Saxony, one of many places claiming to be the sorcerer's birthplace.

(10) 'zitieren': 'conjure up'.

(14) 'Mephistophiles': name of the evil spirit who tempts Faustus. The word may be a corruption of the Greek for 'enemy of light'.

(23) 'schieben': (here) 'shoot'.

(25) 'Post': 'stage coach'.

(49) 'Stadt Portugal': city of Porto Cale (Porto) from which the country derives its name.

(56–68) The theme of Mephistophiles' limitations is broached.

(69–78) As in the *Volksbuch*, the devil himself advises against the pact, thus emphasising the enormity of Faustus' misdeeds.

(81–6) At this point, Faustus is *almost* converted.

(90) Towards the end of the *Volksbuch*, Faustus is described as leading a 'swinish and epicurean life', and Helen of Troy figures as the ultimate temptress. These events are hinted at in the 'Venusbild'

[123]

which here sets the seal on Faustus' damnation.

Further Reading. Alexander Tille, 'Das katholische Fauststück, die Faustkomödienballade und das Zillertaler Doktor-Faustus-Spiel', *Zeitschrift für Bücherfreunde* 10 (1906/7), pp. 129–79; John Meier, 'Die älteste Volksballade von Dr. Faust', *Jahrbuch für Volksliedforschung* 6 (1939), pp. 1–31.

'Wenn ich ein Vöglein wär' (I, 231). Published as 'Der Flug der Liebe' in Herder's *Volkslieder* (vol. I, 1778). One of the most famous German folk songs, it was well-known in the eighteenth century, when it was sung to a melody Herder describes as 'leicht und sehnend'. Its simple rhythm and powerful expression both of intense yearning and of resignation have commended it to posterity. Goethe speaks of it as 'einzig schön und wahr', while Heine sums it up as 'Mondschein, Mondschein die Hülle und Fülle und die ganze Seele übergießend'. Musical settings have been provided by Beethoven, Weber and Schumann.

Further Reading. Walter Naumann, 'Wenn ich ein Vöglein wär', in idem, *Traum und Tradition in der deutschen Lyrik*, Stuttgart, 1966, pp. 9–26.

'Wär ich ein Knab geboren' (II, 29). An example of the 'Grasliedlein' (grazing song, or *pastourelle*). The manuscript suggests it was communicated orally to Brentano, who made a number of alterations. By changing 'Gnäd'ge' (53) to 'Knab', the emphasis is shifted from social to sexual inequality. The 'Reiter' (horseman) becomes a 'Ritter' (knight) in the girl's speech, though her mother continues to speak of him, derisively, as a mere 'Reiter'. Brentano added local colour by emending 'verrauschet' to 'verruschelt' (47, 49). The poem nonetheless rings true; like so many others of its type, it shows a young woman of humble, rustic origin bewailing her disadvantageous position.

(1) 'grasen': 'gather grass'.

(7) 'Ach': misprint for 'Ich'.

(20) 'ab': '[cut] off'.

(25) The dialogue with the horseman suddenly turns into a dialogue between the girl and her mother.

(47, 49) 'verruschelt': (upper German dialect) 'squandered'.

(55) 'rühren': 'beat' (drum).

Further Reading. 'Graserin und Reiter', in *Deutsche Volkslieder mit ihren Melodien*, edited by Deutsches Volkslied Archiv, Freiburg, 1982, vol. 7, pp. 126–55.

'Laß rauschen, Lieb, laß rauschen' (II, 50a). Brentano is thought to have composed this authentic-sounding poem from three distinct sources. Lines 1–4 derive from a 'Grasliedlin' of 1535, and lines 5–12 from a song published by Wolfgang Schmeltzel in *Quodlibet* (Nuremberg, 1544). Lines 13–16 are from a manuscript of uncertain origin, while the last stanza was probably supplied by Brentano, who also composed a musical setting. As Conrady observes, many a successful poem results from fortuitious fusions of this type: 'Manches Lied, das uns als eine glückliche Einheit anmutet, ist mehr oder minder zufällig aus verschiedenen Teilen zusammengewachsen'. It served as a model for Wilhelm Müller's poem 'Wohin' in Schubert's song-cycle *Die schöne Müllerin*. Another version appears in Uhland's *Volkslieder*. Variants are found in all parts of the German-speaking world. The poem's popularity derives from the moving contrast between the relentless swinging of the scythe and the girl's personal grief.

(1) 'Sichlein': 'sickle', '[small] scythe'.

(1) 'rauschen': a favourite word with the Romantics, on account of its onomatopeic properties and vagueness. It can mean 'rustle', 'sigh', 'whisper', 'blow', 'sweep', etc.

(7) 'vertauschen': 'exchange'; Schmeltzel's text reads 'ich hab mir ein pulen [= einen Buhlen] erworben'.

(9) 'worben': 'wooed', 'courted'.

(16) 'verrauscht': (here) 'passes'; a pun on 'rauschen'.

(18) roughly, 'I can't understand what is happening to me'; a phrase suggesting a vague sense of bewilderment or nostalgia.

Further Reading.   Karl Otto Conrady, 'Volkslied — Ich hört ein sichlein rauschen. . .', in Benno von Wiese (ed.), *Die Deutsche Lyrik*, vol. 1 (1957), pp. 99–106; Walter Naumann, 'Ich hört' ein Sichlein rauschen. . .', in idem, *Traum und Tradition in der deutschen Lyrik*, Stuttgart, 1966, pp. 26–37; Charles A. Williams, '*La rauschen, Lieb, la rauschen* and the stanza *Ich hort ein Sichellin rauschen*', *Journal of English and Germanic Philology* 38 (1939), pp. 171–83.

'Ikarus' (II, 161). Sent to Brentano by the Swabian poet Justinus Kerner as a folk poem from Reutlingen in March 1808, this was in all probability written by Kerner himself. It was subsequently published with minor alterations in his *Reiseschatten* (1811) as his own work. The ironic title 'Ikarus' suggests that it was not the invention of an untutored, naive mind, although it uses motifs common to many folk songs.

(1) 'bange': misprint for 'lange'.

(6) 'rennt': misprint for 'weint'.

Further Reading.   Reinhold Steig, 'Justinus Kerners Beziehungen zum Wunderhorn', *Euphorion* 3 (1896), pp. 426–30; Heinz Rölleke, 'Justinus Kerner, Ludwig Uhland und "Des Knaben Wunderhorn"', in Karl-Heinz Schirmer and Bernhard Sowinski (eds.), *Zeiten und Formen in Sprache und Dichtung. Festschrift für Fritz Tschirch*, Cologne, 1972, pp. 278–89.

Ludwig Uhland

Editions

Ludwig Uhland. Werke. Edited by Hartmut Fröschle and Walter Scheffler, 3 vols., Munich, 1980.

Ludwig Uhland. Werke. Edited by Hans R. Schwab, 2 vols., Frankfurt, 1982.

General Reading

Hugo Moser, *Uhlands schwäbische Sagenkunde und die germanistisch-volkskundliche Forschung der Romantik*, Tübingen, 1950.

Hellmut Thomke, *Zeitbewußtsein und Geschichtsauffassung im Werke Uhlands*, Berne, 1962.

Walter Erbe, *Ludwig Uhland als Politiker*, Tübingen, 1962.

Gerhard Storz, *Schwäbische Romantik. Dichter und Dichterkreise im alten Württemberg*, Stuttgart, 1967.

Hartmut Fröschle, *Ludwig Uhland und die Romantik*, Cologne, 1973.

Hugo Moser, 'Ludwig Uhland. Der Dichtergelehrte', in Benno von Wiese (ed.), *Deutsche Dichter der Romantik*. 2nd ed., Berlin, 1983, pp. 563–88.

Life

The early Romantics tended to come from the aristocracy or the wealthy bourgeoisie, and their background is to no small extent reflected in the subjects they chose. Novalis, Brentano, the Schlegel brothers and Tieck showed little interest in examining the lives of ordinary folk. Novalis could be termed a 'poet's poet', and few of the *Märchen* and prose writings of the Schlegels, Tieck and Brentano appear to have been written with the common people in mind. With the publication of *Des Knaben Wunderhorn*, however, interest in folk traditions grew apace, and by 1810 a change from the personal, religious, philosophic and aesthetic aspirations of the first Romantics to more general, practical, popular and political subjects made itself felt. No longer was the Romantic landscape peopled by hermits and knights-errant; peasants and artisans began to appear, the very people whose traditions were documented in *Des Knaben Wunderhorn*. Other poets now began to compile such anthologies themselves; their travels around Germany brought them face to face with the often miserable reality of peasant life, and some became democrats, social critics, and even revolutionaries. Ludwig Uhland may not have been the most militant of these, but he managed to speak out on behalf of the civil rights of the people and combined his career as a writer with service to political causes.

He was born in Tübingen in 1787, entered the local university at the age of 14, and studied law and philosophy for nine years. After a year in Paris acquainting himself with medieval French literature, he was active as a lawyer in Stuttgart and Tübingen, and established a reputation as champion of the rights of the individual. He soon found himself in opposition to the authoritarian organisation of the state of Württemberg, and became a member of the legislative assembly. His first volume of poetry appeared in 1815. He produced an edition of Hölderlin in 1826, and was elected to the Chair of German Language and Literature at Tübingen in 1829, a post which he had to relinquish in 1833, when refused leave to attend political meetings. King Wilhelm of Swabia saw in him a meddling would-be reformer, and wrote, insultingly, 'Sehr gerne Entlassung, da er als Professor ganz unnütz war' on the document accepting his resignation. His admirers, on the other hand, spoke of him as 'das Gewissen Deutschlands'. He lived on as a private scholar and poet, supported by his wife's considerable fortune. Goethe foresaw that his political aspirations would impair his poetic achievements ('Der Politiker wird den Poeten aufzehren'), and Uhland himself admitted that this is what happened. For him, poetry and politics were closely linked to one another. His researches on medieval Germany made him a spokesman of German reunification. He observed the people about and for whom he wrote, and campaigned for improvements in their conditions. Some critics, such as Friedrich Theodor Vischer, claimed that he turned to politics because he was disenchanted with the excessively morbid side of Romantic poetry, but this is hardly a tenable view, since many of his finest poems date from the 1830s, when he was also deeply involved in public causes. His provincialism has also been criticised, but although many of his poems were inspired by Swabian themes and localities, he was quite capable of rising above local issues and drawing inspiration from French, English and other sources. Towards the end of his life, Uhland became increasingly radical, so much so that he was observed on the extreme left in the Frankfurt Assembly of 1848. He refused official honours and decorations, and although fêted by the public on his 75th birthday, there were no official representatives of the state at his funeral a few months later.

[128]

The Poems

'Bauernregel', written 3 December 1807, and 'Hans und Grete', written 28 June 1814, were both published in *Gedichte*, 1815, as short poems illustrating peasant lore and wit. Practical good sense is evident in the former, while the latter, attributed to the rustic-sounding couple 'Hans und Grete', is simple in its vocabulary ('Guckst') and culminates in an unchivalrous but presumably apt repartee.

'Der Wirtin Töchterlein.' Written 24 December 1808, published under the assumed name 'Volker' in *Dichterwald*, 1813. The first couplet recalls numerous folk poems which open with a triadic formula, such as 'Es ritten drei Reiter zum Tor hinaus' (*Des Knaben Wunderhorn* I, 253). Another ballad concerns a mother who promises her daughter to three separate men who then punish her by cutting her into three pieces (*Des Knaben Wunderhorn* II, 200). Romantic motifs include the sharp contrast between life and death (stanza 3), and lasting passion for a dead woman. But the poem may have political implications as well. Since the three men cross the Rhine, it is obvious that the setting is France. Like the innkeeper's daughter whom the youths enquire after, the spirit of freedom kindled nineteen years previously was dead by 1808, crushed by the ensuing chaos and the rise of Napoleon. In this reading, the first two 'Burschen' reluctantly accept the fact of the girl's death, but the third defiantly voices his undying belief in freedom.
  (1) 'Bursche': 'Burschen' (Swabian dialect).
  (8) 'Schrein': 'coffin' (archaic).
  (17) 'hub': 'hob' (archaic).

'Frühlingsglaube.' Written 21 March 1812, published in *Dichterwald*, 1813. The ever-active life-force is contrasted with the sad thoughts of the poet. Faced with the fresh breezes, new sounds and blossoms of spring, he resolves to put his unspecified grief behind him and hope for a better future. Alliteration of 's' and 'w' underlines the idea of a living, breathing life-force behind the manifestations of spring which the poem records ('säuseln', 'weben', 'schaffen', 'blühen'). Numerous musical settings exist, of which the most famous is by Schubert.
  (3) 'an allen Enden': 'wherever you look'.
  (6) 'wenden': 'change' (for the better).

'Frühlingslied des Rezensenten.' Written 19 May 1812, published in *Dichterwald*, 1813. In sharp contrast to the previous poem, the literary critic to whom this satirical piece is attributed (named as 'Spindelmann, der Recensent' in the first version) takes a lukewarm attitude to spring, which he proceeds to review as though it were a book that had just appeared. Grudgingly, he concedes that this season is 'tolerable', 'not too bad' (stanza 3), but it is obvious that he would rather read about spring than experience it directly. The critic had long provided poets (Goethe, Brentano) with a convenient Aunt Sally.

(1) 'ich laß es gelten': critical jargon ('I'll pass it').

(8) 'Meinethalben': 'I raise no objection' (pedantic).

(11) 'Philomele': 'nightingale' (Greek).

(16) 'Kleistens Frühling': Ewald von Kleist's poem 'Der Frühling' (1749), the criterion by which our man of letters proposes to judge the present season.

Further Reading. Hans Mayer, 'Der Kritiker als Poet', in Marcel Reich-Ranicki (ed.), *Frankfurter Anthologie*, Frankfurt, 1977, vol. 2, pp. 34–6.

'Romanze vom Rezensenten'. Written 13 February 1815, published in *Gedichte*, 1815. In this lampoon, believed to be an attack on Christoph Friedrich Weisser, a known opponent of Swabian Romanticism, the critic is compared to Don Quixote. He is the self-appointed protector of the public, here personified as a 'noble lady' (11), against such dangers as the lure of medieval legends, melodious sonnets, and religious verse. These are represented by the dragon, the minstrel and the monk whom he defeats. But modestly, he refuses to be named; his coat of arms remains illegible. The satirical portrait is rounded off with a reference to the honorarium paid to him by his publisher.

(3) 'Andalusien': Andalusia in southern Spain.

(12) 'Siegfriedscher Lindwurm': dragon of the type slain by Siegfried in the medieval epic *Das Nibelungenlied*.

(25) 'Hort': 'comfort'.

'Der Mohn.' Written *c*. 1829, published in *Morgenblatt für gebildete Stände*, November 1829. The poppy plant is the source of opium, and various popular traditions ascribe supernatural powers to it: sleeping in a poppy-field is said to cause disorientation. Uhland draws an analogy between the drugging effect of the poppy and of poetry. Like the madman of stanza 2, the poet of stanza 4 takes his dreams to be as genuine as they are vivid.

(1) 'Westen': the west wind.

(17) 'meiner Tage Morgen': youth.

'Die Ulme zu Hirsau.' Written 1829, published in *Morgenblatt für gebil-*

dete Stände, June 1829. The ruins of the Benedictine Abbey at Hirsau in the Black Forest are the subject of several poems by Uhland and are described by him in letters to Kerner of autumn 1811. Founded around AD 830, and possibly based on an earlier Christian shrine, the monastery was one of the cradles of German Christianity and a centre of learning until its destruction in 1692. The location is described from first-hand knowledge; the elm tree is still to be seen in the midst of the ruins. But the poem's subject is not merely of local interest; Uhland skilfully uses the tree as a symbol of a revitalized Christian faith and also as an emblem of German unity (stanza 8).

(29) 'Wittenberg': university town in Saxony associated with Martin Luther.

'Das Glük von Edenhall.' Written 16 July 1834, published in *Morgenblatt für gebildete Stände*, August 1834. 'The Luck of Eden Hall' was the name of a goblet of enamelled glass kept at Eden Hall in Cumberland, the seat of the Musgrave family. Uhland came across the legend in Ritson's *Fairy Tales* of 1831, but made significant alterations to the material. As in his source, the glass, given to the Musgraves by some fairies, is inscribed with the words 'If this glass do break or fall,/Farewell, the Luck of Eden Hall' (stanza 4). But according to the story, the duke's butler catches the glass in the nick of time and the family are saved. Uhland turns this tale into a parable of arrogance, comparable to Heine's *Belsatzar*, in which the reckless lord challenges fate and is defeated; the butler becomes a voice of caution and good sense. The poem was rendered into English by Henry Wadsworth Longfellow:

> Of Edenhall the youthful Lord
> Bids sound the festal trumpet's call;
> He rises at the banquet board,
> And cries, 'mid the drunken revellers all,
> 'Now bring me the Luck of Edenhall!'
>
> The butler hears the words with pain,
> The house's oldest seneschal,
> Takes slow from its silken cloth again
> The drinking-glass of crystal tall:
> They call it the Luck of Edenhall.
>
> Then said the Lord: 'This glass to praise,
> Fill with red wine from Portugal!'
> The greybeard with trembling hand obeys;

A purple light shines over all,
It beams from the Luck of Edenhall.

Then speaks the Lord, and waves it light:
'This glass of flashing crystal tall
Gave to my sires the Fountain-Sprite;
She wrote in it, *If this glass doth fall,*
Farewell then, o Luck of Edenhall!

''Twas right a goblet the fate should be
Of the joyous race of Edenhall!
Deep draughts drink we right willingly;
And willingly ring, with merry call,
Kling! klang! to the Luck of Edenhall.'

First rings it deep, and full, and mild,
Like to the song of a nightingale;
Then like the roar of a torrent wild;
Then mutters at last like the thunder's fall,
The glorious Luck of Edenhall.

'For its keeper takes a race of might,
The fragile goblet of crystal tall;
It has lasted longer than is right;
Kling! klang! with a harder blow than all
Will I try the Luck of Edenhall!'

As the goblet ringing flies apart,
Suddenly cracks the vaulted hall;
And through the rift the wild flames start;
The guests in dust are scattered all,
With the breaking Luck of Edenhall!

In storms the foe with fire and sword;
He in the night had scaled the wall,
Slain by the sword lies the youthful Lord,
But holds in his hand the crystal tall,
The shattered Luck of Edenhall.

On the morrow the butler gropes alone,
The greybeard in the desert hall,
He seeks his Lord's burnt skeleton,
He seeks in the dismal ruin's fall
The shards of the Luck of Edenhall.

'The stone wall', saith he, 'doth fall aside,
Down must the stately columns fall;

[132]

Glass is this earth's Luck and Pride;
In atoms shall fall this earthly ball
One day like the Luck of Edenhall!'

Joseph von Eichendorff

Editions

Joseph von Eichendorff: Sämtliche Werke. Historisch-kritische Ausgabe. Founded by W. Kosch and A. Sauer, edited by Hermann Kunisch, Stuttgart (in progress).

Joseph von Eichendorff. Werke und Schriften. Edited by Gerhard Baumann and Siegfried Grosse, 4 vols., Stuttgart, 1957–8.

Joseph von Eichendorff. Sämtliche Werke. Edited by Jost Perfahl and Ansgar Hillach, 3 vols., Munich, 1970.

Joseph von Eichendorff. Werke in vier Bänden. Edited by Wolfdietrich Rasch, Munich, 1981.

General Reading

Rudolf Haller, *Eichendorffs Balladenwerk*, Berne, 1962.

Paul Stöcklein, *Joseph von Eichendorff*, Reinbek, 1963 (rowohlts monographien 84).

Oskar Seidlin, *Versuche über Eichendorff*, Göttingen, 1965.

Paul Stöcklein (ed.), *Eichendorff heute. Stimmen der Forschung mit einer Bibliographie*, 2nd ed., Munich, 1966.

Egon Schwarz, *Joseph von Eichendorff*, New York, 1972.

Wolfgang Frühwald, *Eichendorff-Chronik. Daten zu Leben und Werk*, Munich, 1977.

Life

Joseph Freiherr von Eichendorff was born into the impoverished rural aristocracy of Upper Silesia in 1788. Schloß Lubowitz, the ancestral home, provided the setting for a carefree childhood, during which his education was entrusted to members of the Catholic clergy. By the early years of the nineteenth century, the family faced financial problems which were to lead to considerable hardship and eventually to the sale of their estate. After studying law at the universities of Halle and Heidelberg, Eichendorff settled down to the outwardly unsensational life of a civil servant, moving from one administrative centre to another: Vienna, Breslau, Danzig, Königsberg and Berlin. His first novel, *Ahnung und Gegenwart*, appeared in 1815, incorporating around fifty poems, and it was followed by several *Novellen* and a second novel, *Dichter und ihre Gesellen* (1834). A substantial collection of verse appeared in 1837. After his retirement in 1844, he devoted himself to the compilation of surveys of German literature.

Eichendorff's poetic work has, without any doubt, been more popular with the general public than that of Novalis or Brentano. His lyrical output has often been cited as typifying the best qualities of German Romanticism: it is unpretentious, eminently melodic, and has a sound ethical basis. Eichendorff normally manages to combine the simplicity of the folk song with an attitude of natural piety. His works make few demands on the reader; it is easy to follow the narrative line of his stories, such as the much-acclaimed *Aus dem Leben eines Taugenichts* of 1826, or to surrender oneself to the musical lilt of his poems, many of which were made popular through musical settings by Mendelssohn, Schumann, Wolf, and others. Against this, it has to be admitted that his range of subjects is limited and that his treatment of them verges on the trivial. His rhyming technique is as predictable as his imagery is repetitive. It would seem that what was a matter of intense personal passion for Novalis and Brentano had become, for Eichendorff, a routine exercise doggedly carried out with little genuine development either of his style or of his ideas.

What can be said in defence of reading him today? Seidlin has argued that his landscapes constitute a kind of 'visible theology', in which he enacts the basic situations of a religious existence, 'quest and home-coming, threat of temptation and hope of salvation, nearness to and distance from God'. It is certainly possible to look behind the veneer of pleasing formulations and naive optimism, and to recognise in many of his recurring symbols a critical response to the predicament of modern man. Themes such as leave-taking, apprehension, deceit, and ungratified yearning show us a flawed world in which man is all too often denied the fulfilment of his fundamental, legitimate aspirations. Avoidance of political topics and social problems such as feature regularly in Chamisso, Uhland, and Heine is, in Eichendorff, perhaps not so much a sign of indifference as a gesture of resignation in the face of intolerance and repression. Extensively used symbols, such as the cell, the tower, and the walled garden, however idyllic the context in which they appear, reveal a world in which the individual is hedged in, indeed locked away, from real experience. Beauty, as perceived by Eichendorff, is transitory, and the superficially happy world he portrays is constantly threatened by the forces of decay and corruption. Far from urging men to escape into an artificial realm of dreams, Eichendorff may be issuing a cryptic warning to his readers not to give themselves over to their fantasies at the expense of ignoring reality.

[135]

The Poems

'Abschied', written in October 1810, published in *Ahnung und Gegenwart*. One of many poems in which partings occur and farewells are said. The original title was 'An den Hasengarten', a reference to the park at Lubowitz. But Eichendorff preferred to suppress personal reminiscences and the names of specific localities in later editions of his poems; this one becomes 'Im Walde bei Lubowitz' in *Aus dem Leben eines Taugenichts*, 'Im Walde der Heimat' (*Der Gesellschafter*, 1826), and receives its final title in *Gedichte*, 1837.

(5f.) 'out there, the busy world rushes on, forever deceived', a typically summary dismissal of the real world.

(11) 'lustig schlagen': 'sing out cheerfully', one of many clichés often encountered in Eichendorff.

(15) 'auferstehen': the notion of achieving an inner 'rebirth' in Nature.

(20) 'Hort': 'hoard' of (spiritual) treasure, 'consolation'.

'Das zerbrochene Ringlein.' Written *c.* 1810, published in *Deutscher Dichterwald*, 1813, as 'Lied'. Sometimes described as a ballad despite its tenuous story-line, the poem succeeds in recreating the atmosphere of the popular folk song. The mill-wheel, the broken ring, the girl's betrayal are spoken of in the simplest possible way, and the man's desire for escape, be it in the guise of a minstrel or as a soldier, culminates in the despairing suggestion that his unhappiness will only be overcome through death. Musical setting by Friedrich Glück.

Further Reading. Johannes Bolte, 'Das Ringlein sprang entzwei', *Zeitschrift für Volkskunde* 20 (1910), pp. 66–71.

'Zwielicht'. Written *c.* 1815, published in *Ahnung und Gegenwart*. Friedrich, the hero of the novel, hears it sung while on a solitary mountain. A sombre warning against deceit, in which darkness, clouds, and the eerie movements of the trees produce a pathetic fallacy, reflecting the poet's misgivings in a visible form.

(5) 'Reh': 'doe', a popular metaphor for the beloved.

(16) 'bleib wach und munter': compare 1 Thess. 5:6, 'lasset uns wachen und nüchtern sein'.

'Der frohe Wandersmann.' Written before 1817, published in the first chapter of *Aus dem Leben eines Taugenichts*, as an overture to the theme of wandering. Sung to a rousing setting by Theodor Fröhlich, it became a favourite with the ramblers of the *Wandervogel* movement at the turn of this century. Again, it makes few intellectual demands on the reader. The works of the Lord are praised, the stay-at-homes are derided, and the last two stanzas express a spirit of relentless optimism. Parodies, such as the lines 'Wem Gott will rechte Gunst erweisen,/Den schickt er in die Wurstfabrik,/Den läßt er an der Blutwurst beißen,/Und gleich 'n ganzes großes Stück', have been circulating for over a century (Hans Ernst Müller, 'Parodien aus der Schule', *Hessische Blätter für Volkskunde* 12 (1913), pp. 132–9).

(13) Compare the Baroque hymn by Georg Neumark (1621–81): 'Wer nur den lieben Gott läßt walten'.

'Sehnsucht.' Published in *Dichter und ihre Gesellen*, where it is sung spontaneously by Fiametta. A textbook example of motifs generating nostalgia and *Wanderlust*: stars, windows, the coachman's horn, remote forests and springs, gardens and palaces, the music of lutes, and mysterious damsels. The context of the novel, and the marble statues of stanza 3, suggest an Italian landscape, and the poem contains several echoes of Goethe's 'Kennst du das Land, wo die Zitronen blühn?' Structurally, the poem is in two halves. The first (lines 1–12) focuses on the feelings of the solitary figure by the window, while the second summarises the no less intense yearnings of the young travellers.

(5) 'entbrennte': (archaic) 'entbrannte'.

(9) 'Gesellen': 'journeymen'. On completion of their apprenticeship, craftsmen were obliged to spend a specified period gaining practical experience in various places away from home.

Further Reading. Wolfgang Frühwald, 'Die Poesie und der poetische Mensch. Zu Eichendorffs Gedicht *Sehnsucht*', in Wulf Segebrecht (ed.), *Gedichte und Interpretationen III: Klassik und Romantik*. Stuttgart, 1984, pp. 381–93.

'Wünschelrute.' Written in 1835, published in *Deutscher Musen-Almanach*, 1838. A poem in which Eichendorff expresses what many would take to be the true spirit of Romanticism: the poet's unique ability to distil harmony from the ordinary objects of the world by means of a magic formula known only to him.

(1) The potential that lies dormant in everyday things.

(4) 'Triffst': 'if' or 'when' you hit upon [the magic word].

'Zauberblick'. Published in *Gedichte*, 1837. The fatal attraction of a mysterious female was treated by Brentano and by Heine in their earlier poems on the 'Lorelei' theme. Eichendorff offers us a characteris-

[137]

tic variation which shows signs of his familiarity with Heine, in the woman's golden hair (17), and the poet's uncertainty as to the experience (25f.). Suspense is slowly built up, as the poet describes the ruined castle and its surroundings, and is captivated by the magnetic attraction of the figure in the window. His sudden awakening (22) is an ironic device, but in the final stanza Eichendorff stresses not the elusiveness of the dream, as Heine might have done, but its continuing effect on him.

(12) 'Erker': 'oriel' (window).

Heinrich Heine

Editions

Heinrich Heine. Werke, Briefwechsel, Lebenszeugnisse (Säkularausgabe). Edited by Nationale Forschungs- und Gedenkstätten (Weimar) and Centre National de la Recherche Scientifique (Paris), Berlin (East) 1970– (in progress).

Heinrich Heine. Historisch-kritische Gesamtausgabe der Werke (Düsseldorfer Ausgabe). Edited by Manfred Windfuhr, Hamburg, 1973– (in progress).

Heinrich Heine. Sämtliche Schriften. Edited by Klaus Briegleb, Munich 1969–74; 6 vols., repr. Frankfurt, 1981, 12 vols.

Heinrich Heine. Sämtliche Werke. Edited by Werner Vortriede and Uwe Schweikert, Munich, 1969–72, 4 vols.

Heinrich Heine. Werke. Edited by Stuart Atkins, 2 vols., Munich, 1977–8.

General Reading

E. M. Butler, *Heinrich Heine. A Biography*, London, 1956.

Ludwig Marcuse, *Heinrich Heine*, Reinbek, 1960 (rowohlts monographien 41).

Siegbert Salomon Prawer, *Heine. The Tragic Satirist*, Cambridge, 1961.

Eberhard Galley, *Heinrich Heine*. Stuttgart, 1963.

Jeffrey L. Sammons, *Heinrich Heine. A Modern Biography*, Princeton, 1969.

Wolfgang Preisendanz, *Heinrich Heine. Werkstrukturen und Epochenbezüge*, Munich, 1973 (Uni-Taschenbücher 206).

Manfred Windfuhr, *Heinrich Heine. Revolution und Reflexion*, 2nd ed., Stuttgart, 1976.

Fritz J. Raddatz, *Heine. Ein deutsches Märchen*, Hamburg, 1977.

Jürgen Brummack (ed.), *Heinrich Heine. Epoche — Werk — Wirkung*, Munich, 1980.

Hanna Spencer, *Heinrich Heine*, Boston, 1982.

Life

Heine's position within the Romantic movement is less certain than that of the preceding poets. He was a relative latecomer to the movement, and a number of biographical factors (his Jewish origins and the twenty-five years he spent in Paris) have been used to question his standing as a German poet. His work as a journalist, his satirical epics and pamphlets are evidence of an acute perception of social ills and human hypocrisy; his books were banned not only during this century by the National Socialists, but as early as 10 December 1835, when his name headed a list of writers of the *Junges Deutschland* movement whose works were summarily proscribed by the parliament of the day. Conversely, Heine is more widely known and appreciated abroad than any other poet of nineteenth-century Germany. He was more forward-looking and more cosmopolitan than any of his contemporaries, combining in his verse a mastery of the German language at its most musical with subtle attention to social and political issues. But for all his interest in the topical, Heine remained on the political side-lines, preferring to chronicle the foibles of his time rather than to offer constructive criticism. A master of the nuances of Romantic sentiment, he manages to mask his own attitude behind a variety of poetic *personae*. His ironic detachment, as well as his playful exuberance and virtuosity, account for the stimulating effect which his poetry and prose have had on numerous later writers and satirists, from the humorist Wilhelm Busch to the philosopher Friedrich Nietzsche.

Originally destined to become a businessman like his father, Heine proved unable to grasp the essentials of a commercial career and the firm in which his uncle Salomon set him up in 1818 went into liquidation in a matter of months. Thereafter he studied law at the universities of Bonn, Göttingen, and Berlin, and made the acquaintance of August Schlegel, Chamisso, and Goethe. The Romantic metres and motifs which he borrows in his early poetry conceal the un- and often anti-Romantic feelings of the young Heine, crossed in love by his cousin Amalie, and made increasingly aware of antisemitism in the German society of his day, as well as of its many injustices and hypocrisies. Repeated holidays on the North Sea coast and islands were a source of solace and inspiration to him; the *Nordsee* cycle of poems in his *Buch der Lieder* of 1827 combines many of the strongest qualities of his verse: musicality, keen observation and humour.

France had always played an important role in his life; his native Düsseldorf was held by the French in 1795, and again from 1806 until 1813. These military occupations provided, paradoxically, a more equitable, centralised judicial and educational system for the population in general than they had hitherto enjoyed, and particular advantages, such as freedom of movement and settlement, for the Jewish community. Although baptised in 1825, Heine failed to find employment in Germany, even after obtaining a doctorate in law. But the accounts he published of his travels, at home and abroad, were widely acclaimed as highly entertaining and perceptive. He spent four months in England in 1827 and visited Italy in the following year. When he arrived in France in 1831, he was neither an exile nor an emigré but, initially, an established writer of travelogues in search of new material. He rapidly took root in his new environment, working not only as a journalist but also as a tireless, if provocative and subjective, interpreter of German history, philosophy, and literature (see especially *Die romantische Schule*, 1833). After the ban that was imposed on him — but never fully enforced — he received a pension from a secret French government fund, and moved in emigré circles, where he became friendly with progressive thinkers, including Karl Marx. Two mordantly satirical epic poems, *Atta Troll* and *Deutschland. Ein Wintermärchen*, contributed to his increasing notoriety in Germany. In 1848, he was found to be suffering from spinal tuberculosis, and the last eight years of his life were spent confined to his sickroom, where he remained mentally alert despite his increasing paralysis and wrote a substantial number of poignant poems combining bitter sarcasm, wry humour, and touching sentiment.

The Poems

'Belsatzar.' Probably written around 1820, published in *Gedichte*, 1822, no. 10 of the 'Romanzen' section of 'Junge Leiden', the first part of *Buch der Lieder*. A. W. Schlegel had defined the *Romanze* as 'eine romantische Darstellung in volksmäßiger Weise'. The most obvious source is Chapter 5 of the Old Testament Book of Daniel, although in one account Heine claims to have written it before he was sixteen, inspired to do so by the opening line of a Hebrew Passover hymn. Another influence may have been Byron's poem 'Vision of Belshazzar'; both poets omit to mention Daniel himself and concentrate on events rather than on the figure of the prophet. The form of the poem is particularly compelling. The short, self-contained couplets slowly build up to a powerful crescendo: static concepts ('Ruh', 'lag', 'saßen') give way to noise and movement ('schäumend', 'gellend'), and the harsh, masculine rhymes contribute to the sombre atmosphere.

(3) 'Königs': The word and its compounds occur no less than eleven times in the poem, sometimes, as here and in the following couplet, in a parallel formulation. The repetitions are typical of folk poetry in general and of the Old Testament in particular.

(39) 'Die Magier', 'the soothsayers'. Daniel's interpretation of the mysterious words, as reported in the Bible, is ignored.

[141]

'Im wunderschönen Monat Mai.' Written in 1821, published in *Buch der Lieder*, 1827, as the opening poem of the 'Lyrisches Intermezzo' section. Few poems succeed in making the equation of spring with love as succinctly as this does. All details surrounding the basic situation are left to the imagination; the (unrevealed) consequences of the poet's 'confession' could conceivably include anything from an act of love to a slap in the face.

(1, 5) The repetition of the first line may seem artificial, but it is a device encountered in much Romantic verse. The poet was probably familiar with Friedrich Raßmann's 'Einzwängung des Frühlings' (published 1821), which begins 'Im wunderschönen Monat Mai/War ich in einer Bücherei'; Heine was by no means the originator of the ironic use of stock-in-trade images.

'Ein Fichtenbaum steht einsam.' Written in the spring of 1822, published in *Tragödien, nebst einem lyrischen Intermezzo*, 1823. 'Lyrisches Intermezzo' 33. A favourite with Heine's public and especially with his composers. According to Challier's catalogue of *Lieder*, there have been 121 different musical settings. The poem can be read on several levels: as an expression of Romantic nostalgia for the unattainable, as an observation of the paradoxical nature of life and the fatal attraction of opposites, or as an autobiographical comment, in which Heine laments either his separation from his cousin Amalie or, more relevantly perhaps, his own inner dividedness, the 'Fichtenbaum' symbolising the German-Christian layer of his personality, and the palm tree representing the exotic or the Jewish component.

(5) 'Palme': The palm is a biblical symbol of female beauty, e.g. in the Song of Solomon, 7:7.

Further Reading. Philipp F. Veit, 'Fichtenbaum und Palme', *Germanic Review* 51 (1976), pp. 13–27.

'Ein Jüngling liebt ein Mädchen.' Written in 1822, published in *Der Gesellschafter*, 9 October 1822. 'Lyrisches Intermezzo' no. 39. A love poem both abstract and personal; Heine's cousin Amalie spurned him but was herself spurned by the man she loved. Several distancing features, especially the anonymity of phrases such as 'der andre', 'den ersten besten', 'die alte Geschichte', reduce the sparse plot to the level of an epigram. The combination of the banal ('ist übel dran') and the sentimental and rhetorical ('bricht das Herz entzwei', 'just') is typical of Heine's perspective, in which the commonplace is often inseparable from the individual.

(9) 'eine alte Geschichte': Heine uses the same phrase to describe his rejection by Amalie in a letter to Straube of March 1821.

'Aus alten Märchen winkt es.' Written in the spring of 1822, published in *Rheinische Erholungsblätter*, 20 March 1822. 'Lyrisches Intermezzo' 43. Dedicated to Eugen von Breza, who had to leave Prussia for Poland to escape from police persecution for his membership of the proscribed student fraternity Polonia, the poem emphasises the antithetical relationship between beauty as pursued by the Romantics and reality. A political message is clearly encoded into the plea for freedom (20). The motif of the 'rude awakening' after a particularly memorable vision underlines the differences between sorry reality and the poet's ideal. An element of parody is discernible in the repetition of 'wundersüß' (15f.).

(3) 'singt', 'klingt': the slightly overdone internal assonance suggests an excessive employment of beautiful sounds in Romantic poetry and prose.

(5ff.) 'Blumen. . .Mit bräutlichem Gesicht': possibly a reminiscence of the 'blue flower' with the face of a girl in *Heinrich von Ofterdingen*.

'Sie saßen und tranken am Teetisch.' Written late in 1822, published in *Tragödien, nebst einem lyrischen Intermezzo*, 1823. 'Lyrisches Intermezzo' 50. Several members of fashionable society are grouped together around a tea-table, chatting about the meaning of love. The definitions and comments they provide are as false as they are penetrating comments on the hypocrisy of the speakers. 'Never have the pretensions of a materialistic society been more witheringly exposed', writes Siegbert Prawer. The situation is a modern replica in miniature of Plato's *Symposium*, with the figures providing a succession of brilliantly satirical cameo portraits.

(1, 3) 'Teetisch', 'ästhetisch': sloppy, incongruous rhymes, such as Heine will have encountered in Byron, illustrate the artificiality and pomposity of the arguments.

(6, 9) 'Hofrat', 'Domherr': 'Court Counsellor', 'Chapter Canon', honorary titles of little actual significance.

(19f.) 'so hübsch': the ironic point is probably not that the poet's beloved would have provided a more valid verbal definition of love, but that true love *cannot* be defined through words alone, least of all within the framework of fashionable society as it is represented here. Sammons makes the curious suggestion that the poet is castigating his 'Schätzchen' on the grounds that 'she, too, would have taken part in the stupid palaver'.

Further Reading. Jürgen Brummack: 'Heines Entwicklung zum satirischen Dichter', *Deutsche Vierteljahrsschrift für Literaturwissenschaft und Geistesgeschicte* 41 (1967), pp. 98–116.

'Ich weiß nicht, was soll es bedeuten.' Written 1823/4, published in *Der Gesellschafter*, 26 March 1824. 'Die Heimkehr' 2. For the background to the tradition, see Brentano, 'Lore Lay'. After Brentano many Romantics, including Eichendorff and Loeben, wrote poems about the legendary enchantress on the bank of the Rhine. In contrast to the majority of these, Heine's Loreley is not so much a witch as a young woman of great beauty; the sailor is destroyed not by a magic spell or even by his love for the woman, but by the captivating effect of her singing. The event is related as a half-forgotten legend, as if the poet himself cannot be sure of the details (21f.) — one of several distancing effects that make it impossible to separate the voice of the modern, retrospective poet from that of his ancient source. The haunting musical setting by Friedrich Silcher (1837) did much to ensure the poem's popularity — in spite of the composer's textual emendations.

(1) 'Ich weiß nicht . . .': a formula encountered in several poems in *Des Knaben Wunderhorn* (II, 61; III, 17), which can also be read as an alienating device introduced by the modern, sceptical poet.

(12,13) The earlier forms 'goldnes', 'goldnem', were emended to 'goldenes', 'goldenem' after 1844.

(16) 'Melodei': 'Melodie' (archaic).

Further Reading. Ursula Jaspersen, 'Heinrich Heine. "Ich weiß nicht, was soll es bedeuten"', in Benno von Wiese (ed.), *Die Deutsche Lyrik*, Düsseldorf, 1956, pp. 128–33; Heinz Politzer, 'Das Schweigen der Sirenen', *Deutsche Vierteljahrsschrift für Literaturwissenschaft und Geistesgeschichte* 41 (1967), pp. 444–67; Dieter Arendt, 'Ein Märchen aus alten Zeiten. . . ', *Heine-Jahrbuch* 8 (1969), pp. 3–20; Heinz Wetzel, 'Heinrich Heines Lorelei', *Germanisch-Romanische Monatsschrift* 20 (1970), pp. 42–54; Jürgen Kolbe, *Ich weiß nicht was soll es bedeuten*, Munich, 1976.

'Meeresstile.' Written *c.* 1825; published in *Reisebilder*, 1826. 'Die Nordsee. Erster Zyklus' 9. In accute contrast to the epic breadth of the opening stanza, the poem depicts the dirt and meanness of today's mariners and draws an amusing parallel between the thieving cabinboy and the predatory seagull. The title itself is ironic: life at sea is shown to be anything but calm.

(10) 'wehmütig': the boy's sorrow is not soulful *Weltschmerz*, as we

initially assume, but a response to the captain's anger (15f.).

'Das Fräulein stand am Meere.' Written *c*. August 1832, published in *Der Freimütige*, 1833. An epigrammatic poem, in which Heine wittily contrasts self-centred, 'Romantic' speculation with factual empiricism. The laws of Nature in their majestic simplicity transcend the self-induced grief of the sentimental individual. Addressing the girl in the guise of a world-weary rationalist, the poet advises her to shake off her excessive emotionalism.

(3) 'sehre': pseudo-archaic language, used to expose the falseness of such contrived sentimentality.

(6) 'ein altes Stück': 'old hat'.

Further Reading. Ernst Feise, 'Heine's Poem "Ein Fräulein stand am Meere"', *Modern Language Notes* 70 (1955), pp. 350f.

'Im Mai.' Written in 1853–4, published in *Vermischte Schriften*, 1854. 'Gedichte. . ., die der Augenblick erzeugt, womit ich meine Leiden verscheuche, Gedichte der Agonie': the poems now known collectively as 'Letzte Gedichte' were written in the 'Matratzengruft' to which Heine was confined for eight years. In a letter to his publisher, he speaks of them as 'zu dem Eigentümlichsten gehörend, das ich gegeben'. Like Lenau's 'Herbstgefühl', 'Im Mai' revokes the spirit of elation and optimism that earlier poets had derived from the spring. The world is presented as a place of irreconcilable antitheses, such as the paradoxical clash between 'friends' and their 'evil deeds' in stanza 1. The unbridgeable opposition between the beauty of the external world and the poet's suffering makes him 'almost' (9) long for the realm of Hades, where at least, he surmises, he will not be racked by the 'abominable contrast' (10) between joy and pain.

(9) 'Orkus': 'Underworld' (Greek).

(12) 'stygisch': pertaining to the infernal River Styx.

(14) 'Stymphaliden': 'Stymphalian ones', the brazen birds which Hercules overcame.

(16) 'Cerberus': Hound of Hell.

(19) 'Proserpine': wife of Pluto, Lord of the Underworld.

Further Reading. Werner Noethlich, *Heines letzte Gedichte. Vorarbeiten zu einer historisch-kritischen Ausgabe*, Düsseldorf, 1963.

Nikolaus Lenau

Editions

Nikolaus Lenau. Sämtliche Werke und Briefe. Edited by Eduard Castle, 6 vols., Leipzig, 1910–23.

Nikolaus Lenau. Sämtliche Werke. Edited by Hermann Engelhard, Stuttgart, 1959.

Nikolaus Lenau. Sämtliche Werke und Briefe. Edited by Walter Dietze, 2 vols. Frankfurt, 1971.

General Reading

Heinrich Bischoff, *Nikolaus Lenaus Lyrik. Ihre Geschichte, Chronologie und Textkritik.* Brussels, 1920; repr. Berlin, 1920–1.

József Turóczi-Trostler, *Lenau,* Budapest, 1955; Berlin (East) 1961.

Wolfgang Martens, *Bild und Motiv im Weltschmerz. Studien zur Dichtung Lenaus,* Cologne 1957; repr. 1976.

Hugo Schmidt, *Nikolaus Lenau,* New York, 1971.

Hartmut Steinecke, 'Nikolaus Lenau', in Benno von Wiese (ed.), *Deutsche Dichter des 19. Jahrhunderts,* Berlin, 1979, pp. 403–27.

Hansgeorg Schmidt-Bergmann, *Ästhetismus und Negativität. Studien zum Werk Nikolaus Lenaus,* Frankfurt, 1984.

Richard Dove, 'The Rhetoric of Lament: A Reassessment of Nikolaus Lenau', *Orbis Litterarum* 39 (1984), pp. 230–65.

Life

Franz Nikolaus Niembsch, Edler von Strehlenau, was born into the declining lower nobility of Austria–Hungary. His father died, heavily in debt, at the age of thirty; Nikolaus spent his childhood in rural Hungary, and the influence of this country is unmistakable in his poetry, which is musical and sonorous, but also sombre and expressive of a deep yearning for the simple life of the gypsy. Between 1819 and 1830 he studied a variety of subjects in Vienna: philosophy, agriculture, and medicine. Frequent changes of course were symptomatic of an inborn restlessness, as was his failure to complete his studies. When his grandmother left him her fortune in 1830, he decided to devote himself full-time to his poetry. A disastrous love-affair with Berta Hauer, an undistinguished Viennese girl who bore him a child in 1826, had provided what he called 'das unglückliche Geheimnis meiner Jugend' and rendered him unwilling to enter into further binding

[146]

relationships with women.

He began to publish his poems around 1830, using a pseudonym composed of the last five letters of his surname. In Stuttgart, he won the recognition of Gustav Schwab, then the editor of Cotta's influential *Morgenblatt für gebildete Stände*. The first edition of his collected poems appeared in 1832 and was well received; there were six reprints within the next twelve years. But relations with Schwab were strained after he began courting Schwab's attractive niece Lotte Gmelin, and no one could understand why he seemed determined to 'renounce' the woman he claimed to love. Be it on account of previous experiences, or because he recognised that he would not be able to settle down in the academic circles of Stuttgart and Tübingen in which Lotte moved, Lenau determined to make his escape, which he did in characteristically dramatic fashion. After correcting the proofs of his volume of verse, he set sail for America in 1832, in pursuit of what he termed 'ein poetisches Leben'.

It took him four months to travel to Baltimore. There was a collision outside Amsterdam, the company that was to have provided the passengers with land went bankrupt, and the ship barely survived the crossing. Although he purchased 400 acres of land in Lisbon, Ohio, Lenau was soon disappointed: 'Bruder, diese Amerikaner sind himmelanstinkende Krämerseelen. Tot für alles geistige Leben, maustot. Die Nachtigall hat recht, daß sie bei diesen Wichten nicht einkehrt', he wrote to his brother-in-law. There was little trace of the life he had hoped to find roaming through virgin forests and shooting grizzly bears. After a quick tour of the country, he decided he preferred wine to cider and nightingales to mocking-birds, and was back in Germany in June 1833. It was the story of his life. Lenau spent the remaining years before his collapse writing poetry, editing an unsuccessful journal, travelling frenetically between Vienna and Stuttgart, and playing his guitar and violin. Apart from a profusion of short lyrical poems, he is remembered for three works: the lyrical drama, *Faust*, and two epics, *Die Albigenser* and *Savonarola*. *Faust* was published in 1835, but not performed until 1954.

The events of the remaining years of the poet's life reveal a man almost consciously bent on destroying himself. He fell in love with a married woman, Sophie Löwenthal, who repulsed his attentions, but became hysterically jealous if she suspected him of flirting with anyone else. Not until 1844 was he able to detach himself from her influence, at least to the extent of becoming engaged to a Frankfurt woman, Marie

Behrends. He wrote passionate letters to both women, full of ominous references to aches and pains that were attacking him like swarms of black ravens. In September 1844 he suffered a stroke. Marie made her way to Stuttgart to meet him prior to their wedding, but while on the journey she read that Lenau had gone mad and been transported to an asylum in a strait-jacket. He lived for another six years while his faculties deteriorated steadily.

Lenau is remembered for his short, lyrical poems, which are concise, vivid, and musical. Powerfully evocative of a yearning for a simple and natural life, they appealed to the public of the 1830s partly because of their skilful handling of Romantic themes (nostalgia, the outsider, autumnal scenes and portents of death), and because of the intense and genuine emotion that lies behind them. Lenau combines the other-worldliness of Novalis with the passion of Brentano and the observational powers of Chamisso. In common with the late Romantics, he pays considerable attention to accurate descriptions and scene-setting, and is not afraid to discuss sensitive political topics in his verse ('Am Grabe eines Ministers', 'Abschied. Lied eines Auswanderers'). These qualities, combined with his subjective pessimism, which sees man as suffering, lonely, and oppressed, mark him out as one of the last great Romantics.

The Poems

'Bitte.' written *c.* 1831, published in *Gedichte*, 1832. A short hymnic poem in which Lenau returns to the 'unfathomable' magic of night which had been the subject of Novalis's longings more than a quarter of a century earlier. 'Diese Welt' (6), the world of day, activity, reality, is rejected in favour of the powerful lure of night. The metaphor of the 'eye' suggests a relationship between the human and the cosmic, and if the poem is addressed to Lotte Gmelin, whose 'tiefe blaue Augen' deeply impressed him, Lenau is consciously trying to blur the distinction between the two.

'Der Postillion.' Written in 1832, published in *Morgenblatt für gebildete Stände* in 1833. In May 1832 Lenau travelled by stage coach from Stuttgart to Balingen. The postillion stopped his vehicle by the cemetery at Steinhofen and blew a tune on his horn, explaining that this was by way of a tribute to a dead friend. Lenau planned the poem in Balingen and completed it in Ohio during the following winter. Each stanza is self-contained and tends to come to an abrupt end, suggesting a tight control, as if Lenau were unwilling to surrender himself to the atmosphere of nostalgia. The coachman's use of the present tense contrasts with the narrative preterite and draws attention to Lenau's main theme: the persistence of memory in a transient world. The fast-moving, vivid stanzas have contributed to its popularity; Chamisso remarked in 1833, 'Der Postillion scheint mir unübertrefflich und voll- kommen'.

(11f.) The 'quiet bedchamber' of the sleeping flowers ('children of spring').

(29f.) 'Mitten. . .innen': 'in the midst of' ('inmitten').

(37) 'Schwager': 'brother-in-law', here 'coachman'.

(59) 'Ob': 'als ob'.

(62) 'Mit vehängtem Zügel': 'giving free rein', to enable the horses to make up for lost time.

Further Reading. Eugen Flad, 'Lenaus "Postillion" und Steinhofen bei Hechingen', *Eichendorff-Kalender* 1927/8; Werner Weber, 'Lenau', in idem, *Tagebuch eines Lesers. Bemerkungen und Aufsätze zur Literatur*, Olten, 1965, pp. 51–9.

'Die drei Indianer.' Written *c.* April 1834, published in *Gedichte*, 2nd ed., 1834. Lenau visited the Niagara Falls in March 1833 and was struck by the pathetic condition to which the native Red Indians had been reduced. Like the gypsies of Hungary, they are the exploited outsiders in their own country, a predicament from which death provides the only escape. They meet the challenge with the unflinching determi- nation of the noble savage. The pulsating trochaic metre of the poem accords well with the raging elements, the repeated curses of the Indians, and their unbending resolution.

(9) 'Sterbgestöhne': 'deathly moans', typical of the compounds Lenau invents.

(11) 'his erect posture denying his years'.

(21) 'Bettler. . .erklettert': 'climbed onto. . .as beggars'.

(39) 'sturmesmunter': 'lively despite the storm'.

'Stimmen.' A cycle of four sonnets, written in 1837, published in November 1837 in *Wiener Zeitschrift für Kunst, Literatur, Theater und Mode*, as 'Mahnende Stimmen'. In these poems, Lenau is again dis- tancing himself from some of the principles of Romanticism, both by accepting the formal constraints of the sonnet and by paying close attention to the reproduction of minute details from everyday life, a hallmark of the Biedermeier style which was to supplant Romanticism

[149]

in the poetry of Mörike and Droste-Hülshoff. Underlying the cycle is a deeply felt longing for man's lost innocence.

(I, 6) 'durchgaukelnd': 'flitting fancifully'.

(I, 14) 'heimwärts': Man's spiritual 'home' is the hereafter; cf. IV, 12.

(II, 5) 'Scheide': 'barrier'.

(IV, 1–8) The vowels 'ü' and 'ö' in the rhymes suggest the quiet tones of a lullaby.

'Die drei Zigeuner.' Written 1838, published in *Neue Gedichte*, 1838. Like 'Der Postillion' and 'Die drei Indianer', this poem is based on a real experience. On 21 April 1838, Lenau met three dishevelled gypsies in Vienna, took them to an inn, bought them a meal and asked them to play their instruments. In the poem, he sees himself as a weary traveller whose attention is momentarily captured by an idyll fleetingly glimpsed from the window of a passing carriage. Stanza 5 reveals the underlying paradox of the situation: though their clothes are torn and patched, the three 'defiant', 'free' men are in mocking contrast to worldly preoccupations. The poem moves forward towards a climax; the first gypsy is occupied with his music, the second with his pipe, while the third has gone to sleep. The less they do, it would seem, the greater their contentment. Lenau's cultural pessimism receives its fullest expression in stanza 6, where the attitude of contempt ('verachtet') is presented as a legitimate response to the torments of life ('Qual', 3; 'nachtet', 22). As in 'Der Postillion', the ephemeral experience of the moment gives meaning to the fatiguing journey of life.

(4) 'sandige Heide': the landscape recalls the *puszta* of Hungary.

(8) 'Liedel': Austrian diminutive of 'Lied'.

(14) 'Zimbal': 'dulcimer', an instrument consisting of strings over a sounding board, played with small hammers.

(19f.) 'But in their defiant attitude of freedom they mocked their earthly fate'.

'Herbstgefühl.' Written in 1838–9, published in *Deutscher Musenalmanach*, 1840. While many of the early Romantics sang of the delights of spring, Lenau is remembered for his autumnal verse. More than a dozen of his poems bear titles such as 'Herbstlied', 'Herbstklage', 'Ein Herbstabend', or 'Frühlings Tod'. The experience of transience is fundamental to his writing. Spring is seen as heralding winter and decay, its flowers decorate the grave. A poem entitled 'An ein schönes Mädchen' begins 'Wie die Ros in deinem Haare,/Mädchen, bist du bald verblüht. . . '. In 'Herbstgefühl', an analogy is drawn between the autumnal scenery and the dying moments of a sick man, and the quiet waters of a brook are compared to his friends tiptoeing through the sick man's bedroom. Stanza 3 makes the pathetic fallacy explicit; man must accept his place among the visible and audible lamentations of the natural world.

(9) 'trüber': 'pensive', 'dejected'.

(12) 'eingeschlossen': 'included', but also 'imprisoned'.